7/02
Br

SANTA MARIA PUBLIC LIBRARY

D0455651

**Discarded by
Santa Maria Library**

j 796.08209

Aaseng, Nathan.
Women Olympic champions
c2001.

Guad. Br.   SEP 1 7 2002

BRANCH COPY

GAYLORD MG

Women Olympic Champions

Other Books in the History Makers Series:

Women Olympic Champions

By Nathan Aaseng

Lucent Books
P.O. Box 289011, San Diego, CA 92198-9011

On Cover: (center) Jackie Joyner-Kersee, (top right) Babe Didrikson Zaharias, (bottom right) Nadia Comaneci in 1976, (bottom left) Sonja Henie

Library of Congress Cataloging-in-Publication Data

Aaseng, Nathan.
 Women Olympic Champions / by Nathan Aaseng.
  p. cm. — (History makers)
 Includes bibliographical references and index.
 Summary: Profiles the lives and struggles of female Olympic champions
 including Sonja Henie, Babe Didrikson, Fanny Blankers-Koen, Dawn
 Fraser, Lydia Skoblikova, Nadia Comaneci, and Jackie Joyner-Kersee.
 ISBN 1-56006-709-8 (lib. : alk. paper)
 1. Women athletes—History—Juvenile literature. 2. Olympics—History—
 Juvenile literature. 3. Women athletes—Biography—Juvenile literature.
 [1. Athletes. 2. Women—Biography. 3. Olympics—History.] I. Title. II. Series.
 QV709 .A37 2001
 796'.082'0922—dc21
                                                                00-008751

Copyright 2001 by Lucent Books, Inc.
P.O. Box 289011, San Diego, California 92198-9011

No part of this book may be reproduced or used in any other form or by any
other means, electrical, mechanical, or otherwise, including, but not limited
to, photocopy, recording, or any information storage and retrieval system,
without prior written permission from the publisher.

Printed in the U.S.A.

Contents

The literary form most often referred to as "multiple biography" was perfected in the first century A.D. by Plutarch, a perceptive and talented moralist and historian who hailed from the small town of Chaeronea in central Greece. His most famous work, *Parallel Lives*, consists of a long series of biographies of noteworthy ancient Greek and Roman statesmen and military leaders. Frequently, Plutarch compares a famous Greek to a famous Roman, pointing out similarities in personality and achievements. These expertly constructed and very readable tracts provided later historians and others, including playwrights like Shakespeare, with priceless information about prominent ancient personages and also inspired new generations of writers to tackle the multiple biography genre.

The Lucent History Makers series proudly carries on the venerable tradition handed down from Plutarch. Each volume in the series consists of a set of five to eight biographies of important and influential historical figures who were linked together by a common factor. In *Rulers of Ancient Rome*, for example, all the figures were generals, consuls, or emperors of either the Roman Republic or Empire; while the subjects of *Fighters Against American Slavery*, though they lived in different places and times, all shared the same goal, namely the eradication of human servitude. Mindful that politicians and military leaders are not (and never have been) the only people who shape the course of history, the editors of the series have also included representatives from a wide range of endeavors, including scientists, artists, writers, philosophers, religious leaders, and sports figures.

Each book is intended to give a range of figures—some well known, others less known; some who made a great impact on history, others who made only a small impact. For instance, by making Columbus's initial voyage possible, Spain's Queen Isabella I, featured in *Women Leaders of Nations*, helped to open up the New World to exploration and exploitation by the European powers. Unarguably, therefore, she made a major contribution to a series of events that had momentous consequences for the entire world. By contrast, Catherine II, the eighteenth-century Russian queen, and Golda Meir, the modern Israeli prime minister, did not play roles of global impact; however, their policies and actions significantly influenced the historical development of both their own countries and their regional neighbors. Regardless of their relative importance in the greater historical scheme, all of the figures chronicled in the History Makers series made contributions to posterity; and their public achievements, as well as what is known about their private lives, are presented and evaluated in light of the most recent scholarship.

In addition, each volume in the series is documented and substantiated by a wide array of primary and secondary source quotations. The primary source quotes enliven the text by presenting eyewitness views of the times and culture in which each history maker lived; while the secondary source quotes, taken from the works of respected modern scholars, offer expert elaboration and/ or critical commentary. Each quote is footnoted, demonstrating to the reader exactly where biographers find their information. The footnotes also provide the reader with the means of conducting additional research. Finally, to further guide and illuminate readers, each volume in the series features photographs, two bibliographies, and a comprehensive index.

The History Makers series provides both students engaged in research and more casual readers with informative, enlightening, and entertaining overviews of individuals from a variety of circumstances, professions, and backgrounds. No doubt all of them, whether loved or hated, benevolent or cruel, constructive or destructive, will remain endlessly fascinating to each new generation seeking to identify the forces that shaped their world.

Impact Athletes

The close of the twentieth century prompted a barrage of lists in the sports world. A television network trumpeted its "Fifty Greatest Athletes of the Century" profiles. The National Basketball Association selected the fifty best players in its history. Baseball and football observers selected their All-Star Teams of the Century.

Of course, there is no way of determining for certain who were the best athletes of all time, much less of ranking them in order of success. No one can possibly compare an athlete who played in 1912 with someone who starred long after that. Because there is no method of proving one athlete to be better than another, these lists generally trigger disagreement and endless debate.

Any attempt to name seven women Olympic athletes as the cream of the crop invites similar criticism and debate. Hundreds of brilliant performers have electrified Olympic crowds over the century-plus that the modern Olympics have been running. A strong case can be made that many of those whose stories are not told in this book should have been included.

Any sportswriter would gulp hard before chopping 1960s sprinting sensation Wilma Rudolph and the flamboyant speed queen of the late 1980s, Florence Griffith Joyner, from the book. Tatyana Kazankina of the Soviet Union and Joan Benoit of the United States helped shatter myths about the frailty of their gender in long-distance running. U.S. diver Pat McCormick and East German swimming juggernaut Kornelia Ender both brought home a fistful of gold medals from their Olympic trips. The Goitschel sisters from France provided spectacular thrills on the ski slopes, and Bonnie Blair of the United States did the same on the speed-skating rink. All deserve to be mentioned among the greatest women Olympians.

In winnowing this large field of candidates to the final seven, two main factors were considered. The first was raw performance. The seven athletes in this book performed at a level far above what their predecessors or competitors were able to achieve. Sonja Henie is the only figure skater to win the gold medal in her event three consecutive times. No athlete other than Babe Didrikson has broken Olympic records in all three of the primary activities of track and field: throwing, jumping, and running. Fanny Blankers-Koen was the first person to win four gold medals in a single Olympics. In a sport in which most world-class participants burn out while in their teens, swimmer Dawn Fraser held the gold medal for her favorite event through three Olympics. Lydia Skoblikova won gold medals in all four speed-skating distances, from the shortest sprint to the longest endurance race. Nadia Comaneci stunned the gymnastics establishment with a level of performance so high that their equipment could not even display the score. Jackie Joyner-Kersee trounced her competition in the most demanding of all women's Olympic events, the heptathlon.

Along with performance was the consideration of lasting impact, either on the athlete's event or on the sporting world in general. Sonja Henie revolutionized figure skating by choreographing her entire routine so that it became not so much a demonstration of skating skill as a dance on ice. Babe Didrikson opened the public's eyes to the possibility that women could excel at sports. Fanny Blankers-Koen was the first to show that being a star athlete and being a mother were not incompatible. Nadia Comaneci changed the emphasis in women's gymnastics from graceful and fluid movements to breathtaking, high-risk athletic moves. The long-term impact of Fraser, Skoblikova, and Joyner-Kersee was not as dramatic. Yet they, too, raised the standards of achievement in their events to new levels, pushed the known limits of athletic training, and inspired a generation of young athletes to take up their sports.

U.S. diver Patricia McCormick earned a fistful of Olympic gold medals.

In addition, a third factor had to be considered, that of balance. In order for the book to be representative of women Olympians, it had to include a broad spectrum of athletes from various time periods, nations, and events. The seven chosen span the entire history of the Olympics from the 1920s, when women were first beginning to gain recognition as athletes, through the 1990s. They represent six nations and a wide variety of events from both the Summer and Winter Olympics.

CHAPTER 1

The Struggle for Acceptance

Throughout much of history, many societies have considered competitive games to be primarily the domain of men. Some have excluded women from sports because of a prevailing view that allowing women to take part in vigorous physical competition went against basic human nature. Other reasons for this exclusion have ranged from health concerns to a belief that it was indecent to allow women to appear in public wearing swimsuits, shorts, and other uniforms designed to allow the freedom of movement required by sports.

The ancient Greeks considered sports to be in the realm of manly activities when they set up their Olympic Games in 776 B.C. This series of athletic competitions that included footraces, throwing contests, and

Women were forbidden from participating in or even watching the Olympic Games in ancient Greece.

wrestling matches took place every four years for over twelve hundred years. The Olympics were so important to the Greeks that they even suspended their wars in order to hold the Games. The contestants generally performed in the nude, and the arenas in which the Games were held were off-limits to women. There is evidence that at least at one point in history, a woman found in attendance could be put to death.

But although the Olympic Games were the exclusive privilege of men, even the Greeks did not consider sports to be off-limits to women. Every five years, they held a similar, although much smaller-scale, version of the Olympics for women.

Revival of the Modern Olympics

The modern Olympic Games were the brainchild of a wealthy French aristocrat named Baron Pierre de Coubertin. Near the end of the nineteenth century, he proposed reviving the old Greek tradition of a pageant of athletic contests as a way to promote physical fitness and international cooperation. "I shall burnish a flabby and cramped youth,"[1] he proclaimed. His dream came to pass in 1896, when athletes from about a dozen countries traveled to Greece, the ancient home of the Olympics, for fierce yet friendly competition. In keeping with the ancient Greek tradition, Coubertin proposed that the competition be held every four years.

Despite his bold claim that the Olympics "is to be for everyone with no discrimination on account of birth, caste, financial standing, or occupation,"[2] Coubertin continued the Greek ban on women participants. While he lifted the prohibition against female spectators, all of the official participants in the 1896 Olympics were male.

The rebirth of the Olympics, however, took place at a time when women's athletic contests were gaining acceptance in Europe and the United States. The success of women in breaking into the traditional male domain of sports at the turn of the century was so great that one woman athlete wrote, "With the single exception of the improvement in the legal status of women, their entrance into the realm of sports is the most cheering thing that has happened to them in the century just past."[3]

The growing popularity of women's sports put constant pressure on Coubertin and other Olympic organizers to include them in the Olympics, beginning with the very first competition. In 1896 a Greek woman named Melpomene reportedly petitioned the Games' organizers for permission to enter the marathon, a brand-new race of some twenty-five miles, based on an old Greek legend. When her request was denied, she hid herself off to the side of the starting line and ran parallel to the competitors, out of

The organizing committee for the 1896 Olympics continued the ancient ban on female participants.

sight. Once the field passed out of view of the race officials at the start, she moved onto the race course.

A number of male runners dropped out of the race from overheating and exhaustion, and collapsed under shade trees. They were surprised to see a woman run past them, slowly but doggedly. Melpomene arrived at the Olympic stadium in Athens an hour and a half behind the winner, Spiridon Louis, who had finished in 2 hours, 58 minutes, 50 seconds. When Olympic officials refused to allow her onto the track to finish the course, she ran her last lap outside the stadium.

The Olympics Slowly Open Up

The 1900 Olympics, held in Paris, somehow got around Coubertin's opposition and broke the Olympic tradition of males-only by allowing a total of nineteen women to compete in three sports: tennis, golf, and yachting. These exceptions were allowed only because they were individual sports that well-to-do, respectable women had been playing for years and were considered more a courtship activity than a competitive sport. Charlotte "Chattie" Cooper of Great Britain, a three-time Wimbledon champion, earned the distinction of being the first woman to win an Olympic gold medal by capturing the tennis championship.

In 1902 Madge Syers of Great Britain was allowed to enter an international figure-skating competition against a field of male skaters. Her performance so impressed the judges that she earned second place. Instead of applauding her effort, however, skating officials immediately banned women from figure-skating competition. A storm of protest brought women their own separate championship beginning in 1905.

The principal organizer of the 1904 Olympics in St. Louis, James Sullivan of the United States, preferred the traditional men-only competition. He was quoted as saying that organized sports were "morally a questionable experience for women."[4] As a result, even the tennis and golf events were scratched. The only appearance by women in the St. Louis Olympic Games was in an exhibition of archery.

Golf and archery returned as official events in 1908. But the real breakthrough in women's participation took place in Stockholm, Sweden, in 1912, with the addition of women's swimming. This was the first time the Olympics permitted women to compete in a sport that required tremendous physical effort. Several nations, including the United States, declined to send any female representatives. Among the eleven nations that did, few were willing to provide any financial support. Many of the fifty-seven swimmers who competed—including Australians Fanny Durack and Mina Wylie, the outstanding competitors in the swim events—could not travel with the male competitors from their countries and had to pay their own way.

Charlotte Cooper won the first gold medal earned by a woman; in tennis.

U.S. Attitudes

Although a few of its colleges had been promoting women's sports for several decades, the United States lagged behind even the Olympics in approving organized athletic competition for women. The Amateur Athletic Union (AAU), which was the main governing body of sports in the United States, did not accept women's swimming as a legitimate sport until two years after the 1912 Olympics. One of the main reasons for this reluctance was the prevailing

Archery was one of the events in which women were allowed to compete at the 1908 Olympics.

modesty of the time. Women in the early years of the twentieth century were arrested and charged with indecent exposure if their swimsuits displayed bare legs. The other complaint was that competitive sports did not promote proper feminine values. For the first twenty-four years of the modern Olympics, U.S. officials refused to send women to represent the nation in any sport.

In 1920 a great debate raged over whether this policy should be overturned. The U.S. Olympic Committee and most of the team's coaches did not want to budge on the issue. Swimmer Aileen Riggin explains why: "It was not considered healthy for girls to overexert themselves or to swim as far as a mile. People thought it was a great mistake, that we were ruining our health, that we would never have children, and that we would be sorry for it later on."[5]

In the end, however, the antiwomen faction grudgingly gave in to pressure from women's groups and allowed American swimmers to go to the Olympics in 1920 for the first time.

Fierce Battleground

The addition of the Winter Olympics in 1924 provoked little controversy over women's involvement. The only women's event was figure skating, and since the competition was held in cold outdoor ice arenas, the issue of skimpy clothing did not apply. Furthermore, the ancient Greeks never skated or skied, so there was no concern about breaking tradition.

The fiercest battleground in the struggle over women's Olympic involvement was track and field. These running, throwing, and jumping events provided the core of the original Olympics and were considered the showcase events of the modern Games. During the 1920s, sports organizations put a great deal of pressure on the International Olympic Committee (IOC) to include women's track-and-field events. Even the traditionally conservative U.S. Amateur Athletic Union had been sanctioning women's track-and-field meets since 1916. Female track-and-field athletes began competing in international competition in 1921.

But as long as Pierre de Coubertin remained in charge of the Olympics, he fought off all proposals for women's track and field. To his dying day, Coubertin tried to keep the Olympics as free of women as possible. "Let women do all the sports they wish—but not in public,"[6] he proclaimed.

Coubertin's reign, however, could not last forever. He retired as president of the IOC before the 1928 Olympics. His successor, Count Henri de Baillet-Latour of Belgium, tried to uphold Coubertin's principles, but he did not have the same clout as the Olympic founder. Over his objections, a small number of women's races were included on the 1928 Olympic program in Amsterdam.

The Infamous 800 Meters

One of the women's events in that competition was the 800-meter race. Other than the Germans, who were more accepting than most nations of female athletes, few women of that time had experience at so long a race. They were unwitting victims of Lina Radke and her German teammates' strategy for winning the gold medal. Radke's teammates took off at a blistering pace. The competition strained mightily to keep up with them, while Radke trailed comfortably behind. The front-runners eventually ran themselves into exhaustion, and Radke was able to fly past them at the end with an impressive time of 2 minutes, 16.8 seconds.

Radke's strategy, however, had an unintended, disastrous effect on women's athletics. Almost all the women had pushed themselves to the very limits of their endurance. The result was described in wrenching detail by shocked sportswriters. "Below us on the cinder path were eleven wretched women," wrote one American columnist, "five of whom dropped out before the finish, while five collapsed after reaching the tape."[7]

Instead of being impressed by the women's heroic efforts, many people were appalled. Fred Steers, chairman of the Women's Athletic Committee of the AAU, declared that "the effect and fatigue of competition does not conform to the American ideals of womanly dignity and conduct. It does not lead to the promotion of sport, but on the contrary, because of its effect on the spectators, is detrimental."[8]

People claiming to be medical experts weighed in with their judgment that the 800-meter race was merely proof that women were not physically designed for sports. Some critics claimed that female athletes ran an increased danger of developing heart trouble. Donald A. Laird wrote in *Scientific American* that "feminine muscular development interferes with motherhood."[9]

Even other female athletes had second thoughts about how far women should go in their pursuit of sports opportunities. Betty Robinson, a sprinter who won the United States' first gold medal in women's track and field at the 1928 Games, said in an interview that women were not built for races as long as 800 meters.

Ignored amid the controversy was the fact that medical research showed no ill effects for women from strenuous physical exercise. Also ignored was the fact that men, particularly in rowing races, frequently worked themselves to the edge of consciousness in their events without drawing any particular notice.

Backlash and Boycott

The furor over the 800-meter event touched off a backlash against women's participation in track and field. Immediately following the Olympics, the International Olympic Committee voted to drop women's track and field from the program. IOC president Baillet-Latour tried to eliminate all women's events, and he was supported in this by a number of organizations, including the Women's Athletic Committee of the National AAU in the United States.

Women's track-and-field organizers decided to hold their own World Games following the 1928 Olympics, a practice that continued until 1935. But even the International Amateur Athletic Federation banned all long races from women's competition.

Meanwhile, within all those groups were individuals stubbornly committed to promoting sports competition for women. The most influential of these was Gustave Kirby, who became president of the AAU prior to the 1932 Olympics in Los Angeles. With the support of an unlikely ally, U.S. Olympic administrator Avery Brundage, Kirby declared that the U.S. men's team would boycott the track-and-field events if women were not allowed to compete.

IOC officials recognized this as a serious threat to the future of the Olympics. If the host team, which also boasted many of the world's best athletes, sat out the showcase competition of the Games, the entire affair could be a financial and public relations bust. Despite the strenuous objections of France, England, Italy, and Hungary, the IOC backed down and allowed a limited number of women's track-and-field events at the Los Angeles Olympic Games.

Threatened with a boycott by the U.S. men's team, the IOC allowed women's competition in track-and-field events at the 1932 Olympics.

Tarnished Image

Some of the women gave spectacular performances at the 1932 Olympics, yet even they failed to dislodge widespread public prejudice against female athletes. Track-and-field stars such as sprinter Stella Walsh and all-around performer Babe Didrikson drew criticism because they did not conform to the standards of feminine behavior.

Avery Brundage was one of those offended by the so-called "muscle molls" of sport. Once a supporter of women's Olympic competition, he changed his mind after taking control of the IOC. "You know, the ancient Greeks kept women out of their athletic games," he told reporters. "They wouldn't even let them on the sidelines. I'm not so sure but they were right."[10]

Sportswriters, for the most part, ignored women's athletic competitions. Bert Nelson, a writer for *Track & Field* magazine, explained why in response to a complaint about the lack of coverage: "Personally, I can't get very excited about girlish athletes. . . . I seem to feel about the same as 99 per cent of the track fans I know."[11]

Growing Participation

Despite the opposition of Brundage and others, women's participation in the Olympics grew steadily. Following a twelve-year break caused by World War II, the 1948 Olympics offered an expanded slate of women's track-and-field events. Included was an event previously dismissed as something entirely unfit for women: the shot put. Women's alpine skiing was also added to the Winter Olympic program that year.

The 1952 Helsinki Olympics added a sport that would prove to be one of the most important in popularizing women's athletics—gymnastics. Eight years later, the long-standing misconceptions about women and endurance events finally began to give way under a mountain of contradictory evidence. The 1960 Rome Olympics finally broke the thirty-two-year ban on women's track races longer than half a lap, by bringing back the infamous 800-meter run. That same year, women's speed skating made its Olympic debut at Squaw Valley, including a grueling 3,000-meter race.

Clouds of Suspicion

In the meantime, female Olympic competitors were plagued by suspicions that they were not really women at all. Whenever a woman dominated a particular event, especially if some of her physical features were not particularly feminine, accusations arose that she was a man masquerading as a woman. Some of the suspicions turned out to be accurate. The great sprinter Stella Walsh, a Polish immigrant who grew up in Cleveland, won the gold medal in the 100-meter dash in 1932 with what one reporter referred to as "man-like"[12] strides. But it was not until Walsh was shot to death in a parking lot in December 1980 that the truth came out: an autopsy revealed that Walsh was indeed a man.

The cloud of suspicion that hovered over female Olympic competitors due to impostors like Walsh brought about the use of sex tests in the 1970s. When those tests were instituted, the threat of men competing in women's events disappeared from the Olympic scene. But it was replaced by another cloud of controversy over the use of performance-enhancing drugs. The East German women's teams, which appeared out of nowhere to dominate the Olympics in the late 1970s and 1980s, came under heavy suspicion of drug use. Many competitors complained that powerful athletes such as 5 foot 11 inch, 170-pound swimming sensation Kornelia Ender got their strength not from training but from the pharmacy.

Eventually the East German sports program was exposed for its widespread use of drugs such as steroids that increased athletes' muscle mass. The East German women were both furious and embarrassed at the revelation that they had unknowingly taken these drugs. "Medical men are the guilty people," fumed Ender, upon learning of the fraud. "They gave us things, . . . we were never asked if we wanted them."[13]

Breakthrough

Despite such obstacles, the women's movement in the Olympics continued to flourish. Gradually, the distances women were allowed to run increased. In the 1970s, a 1500-meter race, roughly the equivalent of a mile, was added to the Olympics. The final breakthrough in the battle for recognition of women's athletic capabilities came in 1984, when the Olympics returned to Los Angeles. That year the IOC added the 26.2-mile marathon, the Olympics' most demanding race, to the schedule of women's events. Joan Benoit of the United States proved once and for all that the former notions about the frailty of women were bogus. Despite withering heat and humidity, Benoit completed the course in 2 hours, 24 minutes, 52 seconds.

Stella Walsh sets a world record for the 220-yard run in 1935.

Benoit's time would have shocked the officials of the 1928 Olympics, who declared that an 800-meter race was beyond the ability of women. Not only was Benoit's time better than that of any of the male marathon runners in the 1928 Olympics; she would have finished a mile and a half in front of that year's gold-medal winner. Her performance, and those of the runners who finished close behind her, put to rest for all time the old myths that athletic competition was for men only.

No More Question

At the dawn of the twenty-first century, the debate over women in Olympic competition was dead and buried. Women have become nearly as active in Olympic competition as men. Team sports such as soccer and softball, once thought of as exclusively for men, were included in the women's program for the first time in the 1996 Atlanta Games. The number of female Olympic athletes in Atlanta climbed to more than four thousand.

Perhaps the most telling example of society's change in attitudes toward women in Olympic competition has been television ratings. Beginning in 1992, television networks found that well over half the viewers of their Olympic coverage were women. The days when a sports editor could claim that nobody cared about female athletes was but a distant memory.

CHAPTER 2

Sonja Henie

After watching the frantic mob that swarmed around one of the world's top athletes wherever she went in 1932, a New York sportswriter commented that the object of their affection was "undoubtedly the biggest individual draw sports has ever produced."[14] This statement came from a writer who covered sports in the city where the legendary Babe Ruth was still blasting home runs for the Yankees. What was even more remarkable is that the athlete he was talking about was a woman.

At a time when a fierce debate continued to rage over whether women ought to take part in competitive sports at all, Sonja Henie soared past Ruth, Jim Thorpe, football's Red Grange, and every other male athlete in history to become the most famous and beloved athlete in the world. In the process, she almost single-handedly transformed figure skating from a minor sport to a glamorous athletic showcase. At the same time, she helped elevate the Winter Olympics from a weak imitation of the Summer Games to what has become a major broadcasting spectacle worth hundreds of millions of dollars.

Dreams of Being an Ice Queen

Sonja Henie was born on April 8, 1912, in Kristiania (now Oslo), Norway. She was the younger of two children born to Hans Wilhelm and Selma Henie. When Sonja was very young, her parents took her to see an ice carnival. The effortless magic of gliding on skates so impressed her that she declared her wish to be an ice queen someday. Mrs. Henie told her that if she worked hard and paid close attention to her instructors, she would reach her goal.

However, little more was said about the incident. It seemed just another expression of Sonja's desire to perform before an audience. She loved to dress up in some of her mother's fine clothing and give dance recitals in the living room to any adults she could coax into watching. Her attention to detail was astounding for a girl not yet of kindergarten age: she would make tickets, usher her guests to their seats, and then perform to the music of a record player.

Sonja had the good fortune to grow up in one of Oslo's wealthiest families. Wilhelm was a shrewd businessman who made a fortune as the owner of Norway's largest fur-trading company. He was able to encourage Sonja's interest in dancing by arranging lessons with Love Krohn, Norway's foremost ballet master.

First Pair of Skates

As well as encouraging Sonja in the more traditional pursuit of dance, Wilhelm also encouraged her to take part in a wide variety of sports. He had been an international champion bicycle racer during his younger days and believed strongly in the importance of outdoor physical activity. The family owned a hunting lodge at the mountain village of Gerlo, where they often skied. Sonja learned to ski shortly after learning to walk, determined to keep up with her older brother, Leif.

For some reason, Mr. Henie was more reluctant to let Sonja loose on skates than on skis. Although he told her she was too young for skates, he finally gave in to the six-year-old's begging and let her try a pair of roller skates. The next winter, she tried out her first pair of ice skates.

Sonja at age three with her older brother Leif.

Immediately, however, Sonja detected a difference between the skates she was supposed to wear and those worn by her brother. Hers were training skates that had an extra blade for balance. Leif's were regular skates. Sonja raised a terrible fuss until Mr. Henie reluctantly gave her a pair of skates like Leif's. She fell and bruised herself often on those skates in her attempts to imitate her older brother at the local skating rinks. But her balance was far advanced for her age. Barely a year after beginning to skate and with little instruction other than the tips given by the better skaters at the rink, she began to enter figure-skating contests.

History of Figure Skating

People in northern Europe had been skating for hundreds of years by the time Sonja first laced up a pair of ice skates. Until the sixteenth century, the runners on skates were made of wood that was waxed to provide the desired glide. In 1572 the first iron-bladed skates were introduced. These could be honed to a sharper edge than wood and so allowed the skater to make sharper turns.

Until the late nineteenth century, skating was primarily a recreational activity and occasional winter transportation. The only competitions were in speed skating. The intricate zigzagging and other tricks that skaters sometimes tried were merely for their own amusement.

That began to change shortly after 1850, when E. W. Bushnell of Philadelphia began manufacturing skate blades out of steel. These blades, which were even harder and more durable than iron, spurred great interest in the sport in the United States. Among those who took a serious interest in skating was Jackson Haines, a well-known dancer and ballet instructor. In 1864 Haines immigrated to Vienna, Austria, where he started a school that transferred some of the techniques of dancing to the ice. Haines taught his students to glide on the ice in time with recorded waltz music.

Haines's pupils, who came from a variety of countries, enjoyed the activity immensely. They quickly carried the idea to their homelands. Interest in the new sport grew so much in Canada that enthusiasts there formed a skating club in 1878. Within a decade, skating clubs were popular in many cold-weather countries.

Meanwhile, a different kind of ice-skating had been evolving in England. Ice-skaters in that country had begun setting up competitions to see who could trace the most precise figures on the ice. By the dawn of the twentieth century, the two forms of skating had merged into a two-part competition known as figure skating. Skaters were judged first on their ability to perform precision turns while tracing patterns, and then on their overall skating skill in a performance set to music. This sport was included in the 1908 London Olympics, although for men only.

Early Competition

Sonja was seven years old when she entered her first skating competition. A year later, she entered and won Norway's Junior Class competition. That opened the Henies' eyes as to what their daughter could accomplish. They found a coach for her, Oscar Holte, who marveled at his young student. "I've never seen a little girl so determined to skate, and with the ability to do it with so much sparkle and verve,"[15] said Holte.

Sonja Henie's last-place finish at the 1924 Winter Olympics in Chamonix, France inspired her to work even harder.

Sonja was pulled out of school so that she could put in the hours of practice she needed. For nearly twelve months a year, she skated for three hours in the morning and two hours in the afternoon. The rest of her time was filled with schoolwork, which was taught to her by a private tutor.

The hard work paid off. In 1924 the twelve-year-old Henie won Norway's national figure-skating championship. A few weeks later, she was off to Chamonix, France, to take part in the first Winter Olympics. The little blue-eyed blond from Norway captured the hearts of many of the spectators. John Rendel wrote in the *New York Times* that Henie "traces the most intricate patterns on the ice and executes leaps and spins in the air with a lightness that appears to defy gravity."[16]

The figure-skating judges, however, were not as easily impressed. Henie finished last out of eight competitors, far behind the seventh-place finisher. The defeat only inspired her to try harder. She begged her parents to help her get the best instruction possible. They were willing to spend part of their large fortune sending Sonja and her mother to Germany, England, Switzerland, and Austria, to train under the top coaches in the world. The effort paid off. In 1926 Henie won second place in the World Championships.

Revolutionizing the Sport

At the same time, Henie was beginning to develop her own unique style of skating. The other skaters were basically performing a series of graceful turns, spins, and twirls set to music. Sonja, who had always loved to dance, looked for ways to blend dance techniques with skating. While traveling in Europe to train with the best skating instructors, she also took lessons in ballet from the greatest masters on the continent. Gradually, she began to include in her routine ballet patterns based on those of her favorite ballerina, Anna Pavlova of Russia. Unlike the other skaters, who used the music as nothing more than a pleasant background to their moves, Henie worked hard at choreographing these moves to the music. When she skated her freestyle program, it was as if she were dancing on ice.

Henie also looked for ways to take advantage of her exceptional athletic ability. Not only was she a fine skater and dancer, but she was also an expert horseback rider and swimmer, and so skilled as a tennis player that she once won the Norwegian women's championship in the sport. She used this all-around athletic skill to introduce jumps and spins that no one had ever tried before. Eventually, she included nineteen different types of spins in her program, many of them her own invention.

Her final innovation was a change in clothing. During her early years of competition, she could not perform many of the moves she wanted because of the bulky ankle-length skirts that women wore during competition. Her mother helped her design a new type of outfit with a shorter skirt that gave her far greater freedom of movement. Sonja also discarded the traditional plain black skates in favor of beige and then white. Her stylish new costumes began to attract as much attention as her skating.

A Star Is Born

Henie took a great risk in all three of her innovations. Figure-skating judges were known for being firmly wed to tradition. In 1920 they had severely criticized a U.S. skater named Theresa Weld for including a jump in her program. Jumps, according to the officials, were not ladylike.

At the 1927 World Championships in Oslo, however, Henie carried out her innovative skating program with such stunning grace and artistic beauty that she won over both the spectators and judges, who awarded her first place.

Some of her competitors complained that Henie had been given the benefit of a hometown decision in that competition. But the 1928 Olympics destroyed that notion. Spinning and twirling in perfect rhythm to the music, Henie put on an astounding show that blew away the competition.

Crowds were so impressed that Henie became the biggest international sports star the world had ever seen. During a competition in Göteburg, Sweden, in 1929, she narrowly avoided a serious injury when crowds, pressing in to get a look at her, shattered the windshield of the car she was riding in. Rather than backing off after that close call, the crowd continued to surge after her all the way to her hotel. There, according to news reports, "big plate glass windows were smashed by the crush of humanity, and order was restored only by the arrival of the militia."[17] When the figure-skating World Championships returned to Oslo a few years later, twelve thousand people crammed into the outdoor stadium to see Henie, while another three thousand sat on the surrounding hills despite the freezing weather.

Invincible

When Henie arrived in the United States for the 1932 Olympics in Lake Placid, New York, the press and the fans treated her like a goddess. Crowds followed her everywhere. Sportswriters fed their readers whatever details they could find, including descriptions rarely found on a sports page. One writer went on at length about her costume, the "bewitching salmon-colored velvet . . . edged with fawn-colored fluffy fur, the ensemble topped with a fawn-colored turban."[18]

Despite her status as a living sports legend, Henie never took winning for granted. Convinced that she needed luck to go along with her talent, she refused to take the ice without wearing her lucky rabbit's foot. Included in her collection of custom-made skates was a pair that she never wore; these were her lucky skates, and she made sure they were always present at her competitions.

Sonja Henie (right) is pictured here with Fritzi Burger of Austria. Burger was Henie's closest competition at the 1932 Winter Olympics.

Henie needed no luck in capturing her second consecutive figure-skating gold medal. The 5 foot 2 inch, 110-pound whirlwind jumped higher, spun faster, and skated more gracefully than anyone the crowd had ever seen. Although Fritzi Burger of Austria put on the finest performance of her career, Henie was never in danger of losing her medal. One reporter wrote of her performance, "By so much did she outdistance the field that only one, Miss Burger, could be rated in her class."[19]

Going for a Third

In the history of the Olympics, one of the rarest achievements is winning an event in three consecutive Olympics. Since the Games are held only every four years, an athlete has to remain at his or her peak for nearly a decade to accomplish this.

Helped by the fact that she had started her winning streak while a fairly young teenager, Henie remained firmly atop the skating world as the 1936 Winter Olympics in Garmisch-Partenkirchen, Germany, approached. By this time the twenty-four-year-old Norwegian star had won ten straight World Championships and had seldom been seriously challenged in any of them.

But these Olympics brought with them a pressure unlike any Henie had ever known. Prior to the Games, she had announced her decision to retire from the sport after the competition. Frenzied crowds fought a beefed-up police force to get into the ice arena to watch the final competitive performance of the most popular athlete in the world. Henie, who was never supremely confident even when she was most dominant, fretted over the event. Some of the younger skaters had adopted her techniques and had developed into formidable challengers. What if, in her final moment of glory, in the crowning moment of her career, she failed? What if one of these young skaters stole her medal and sent her into retirement to live the rest of her life with the bitter taste of defeat?

By the time she competed in the 1936 Olympics, Sonja Henie had become the world's most popular athlete.

Concentrating as she never had before, Henie flawlessly traced the figures in the compulsory round of the competition. She hoped this had given her a comfortable cushion over her opponents to relieve some of the unbearable pressure she felt. But as she read the results on the display board, she received a jolt. The judges had put her only 3.6 points ahead of Great Britain's rising teenage star Cecilia Colledge. Henie knew that Colledge considered the freestyle portion of the program, which was yet to come, to be her stronger suit. In fact, Henie had won the previous World Championship over Colledge only because of her edge in the compulsory figures. Furious at the result, her nerves worn to a frazzle, she ripped Colledge's score off the board and tore it to pieces.

Moment of Truth

Colledge was the first to skate in the final round. As a young, perky underdog skating against a legend, she had already captured the sympathy of much of the crowd. She further excited the German audience by offering the Nazi salute to her hosts at the start of her program. After a slight delay because of a problem with the sound system, Colledge took off in her quest to dethrone the champion. Throughout a program of whirls and leaps that rivaled Henie's best, the crowd roared its approval. Finishing to a thundering ovation, Colledge received scores of 5.7 out of a possible 6.0 for both her performance and the level of difficulty in her routine.

Shaken by the clamor over Colledge's performance, Henie skated onto the ice knowing she had little margin for error. Sensing the tension in the star, the crowd looked on in an edgy silence that was all the more nerve-racking in contrast to the raucous greeting given Colledge.

But once the music started, Henie was in control as she had always been. She flew through her routine, every inch the ice queen that she had been for the past ten years. At a time when she needed it most, Henie put on a performance that most experts ranked as her greatest since her first stunning World Championship ten years earlier. The judges awarded her 5.8 for both performance and difficulty. Henie won the gold and went into retirement after being undefeated for over ten years and three Olympics.

Springboard to Success

Henie took advantage of her unprecedented popularity to set up a professional figure-skating tour throughout the world. In addition, she traveled to Hollywood, determined to be a movie star. "I

Sonja Henie in a scene from One in a Million, *one of the twelve successful Hollywood films she starred in.*

want to do with skates what Fred Astaire is doing with dancing," she declared. "No one has ever done it in the movies and I want to!"[20]

She succeeded on both counts, becoming the first athlete, male or female, to earn a million dollars from her talents. Inheriting the business savvy of her father, she at first starred in, and then later produced, successful ice shows. Beginning with the film *One in a Million,* Henie starred in twelve films over a period of twenty years, and at one time became Hollywood's third highest box-office attraction. Her movies and ice shows earned her a staggering amount of money, believed to be somewhere around $50 million.

Her personal life was less successful. Henie married and divorced two American husbands before marrying Norwegian Niels

Onstad and retiring to Norway. In the late 1960s, she developed leukemia and died on a hospital plane en route from Paris to Oslo, on October 12, 1969.

Legacy

In winning ten consecutive World Championships and three consecutive Olympic titles, Sonja Henie left a record unmatched in the world of figure skating, and scarcely matched in any sport. Even more important, however, was her impact on the sport of figure skating, the Olympics, and the future of women's athletics.

As analyst Sandra Stevenson observes, "She revolutionized the sport, changing it from an amusing pastime engaged in by the upper classes in the elite winter watering spots to a highly competitive actively contested sport."[21]

Henie was the first in a long line of dazzling skaters who have made women's figure skating into one of the most popular televised sports events in the world. The star power she provided helped the Winter Olympics, which began as a sideshow to the Summer Olympic Games, develop into a billion-dollar industry. Finally, Henie was the first to prove that women athletes could not only gain respect; they could reach the very pinnacle of international acclaim and adoration.

CHAPTER 3

Babe Didrikson

Melvorne "Colonel" McCombs was proud of the publicity that his Employers Casualty Insurance women's basketball team had brought to the company in the early 1930s. Looking for another way to capitalize on the talents of the athletic young women who had earned a national AAU title, he decided to organize a company track team.

McCombs asked his basketball star, Babe Didrikson, what events she would like to enter. Without hesitating, Didrikson answered, "Well, I'm going to do all of them."[22] She was serious. The idea that there might be a sport, or even an event, at which she could not excel did not even occur to her.

She would learn later that she was living in an era in which Olympic officials had their own ideas of what a woman could do. Although she was the star of the 1932 Olympics, Didrikson could only fume about what she could have accomplished had she not been limited by needless restrictions. "I'd break all the records if only they'd let me,"[23] she said.

Social Outcast

Mildred Ella Didrikson was born on June 26, 1911, to Ole and Hannah Didriksen, a couple who had recently immigrated to Texas from Norway. (She later changed the spelling of her last name.) After years of earning a modest living as a seaman, Ole Didriksen had taken up work as a cabinetmaker in his new country. He used his professional skill to build a gymnasium to keep his seven active children occupied.

The child who appreciated it the most was Mildred, the next-to-youngest child. She became almost obsessed with sports. "Before I was even in my teens I knew exactly what I wanted to be when I grew up," she reflected in later life. "My goal was to be the greatest athlete that ever lived."[24]

The statement reflected Mildred's refusal to concede anything to males in the area of physical activity. Never was she interested in being the best female athlete; she wanted to be better than anybody, male or female. Many a boy at Magnolia Elementary School in Beaumont, Texas, discovered to his sorrow that Mildred would back down from no one. Her reputation as a tomboy who beat up boys made her a social outcast in school.

Focus on the Olympics

Mildred found support for her athletic interests from her father. Ole Didriksen liked to pore over the sports section of the papers and comment on what he saw. Mildred loved joining his discussions. During the summer of 1928, the two closely followed news reports of the Olympic Games held in Amsterdam. Tales of the new women's track events got Mildred so excited that she began to practice running hurdles on her own. There were seven hedges dividing the yards between her house and the corner grocery store.

Babe Didrikson began competing in track-and-field events while an employee of Employers Casualty Insurance.

Basketball was just one of the many sports in which Babe Didrikson excelled.

Mildred decided to turn that end of the block into her own private race course. She ran and hurdled over the hedges, constantly trying to improve her time. Instead of being upset with her for cutting through their yards, the neighbors were supportive. One of them even clipped his hedge to the proper height when Didrikson complained that it had grown too high for her.

While developing her own training routines, Didrikson joined every sport available to her. Texas was ahead of the rest of the nation in allowing women to participate in athletics, and Didrikson was able to compete in baseball, basketball, volleyball, golf, tennis, and swimming while in high school. She once hit five home runs in a single game. This brought comparisons to the current major league home run king Babe Ruth and earned her the life-long nickname of Babe.

Unofficial Pro Athlete

Didrikson's phenomenal success caught the interest of Colonel McCombs of the Employers Casualty Insurance Company in Dallas. In 1930, while Babe was still in high school, he offered her a full-time job as a secretary. His main interest, however, was not in her typing but in her basketball skill. Employers Casualty fielded a women's basketball team that competed nationally, and McCombs believed Didrikson could help boost them to the championship. Babe, who had never cared for school, was happy for the opportunity.

Babe proved to be a dominant player. In her three years with the Golden Cyclones of Employers Casualty, she led the team to three AAU finals and one national title. Behind the celebrating, however, was a team on the verge of civil war. From the start, Didrikson was more of an individual star than a team player, and her teammates came to resent her style of play.

Recognizing that the good times would not last long for a basketball team in such turmoil, the enterprising McCombs searched for a different outlet for his star's talents. Track and field seemed the obvious choice. Didrikson had never given up her dream of competing in the Olympics.

At the women's AAU National Championships in Dallas in 1930, the teenager won both the javelin and baseball throw, and came within a quarter inch of capturing the long-jump title as well. The following summer, she topped that performance at the AAU Nationals in Jersey City, New Jersey. Those days of hurdling the neighbors' hedges paid off as she not only won the 80-meter hurdles but also set a world record. Didrikson followed that success by setting an American record in the baseball throw and capped her afternoon by winning the long jump.

One-Woman Team

Didrikson's amazing performance and her determination to succeed at every event possible gave McCombs an idea. What if Babe was so good that she could single-handedly win the national team title in track? The publicity from such an accomplishment would be staggering.

Unfortunately, AAU rules allowed a woman to take part in only three track-and-field events. McCombs persuaded officials to waive the rule by pointing out the public relations value of one superwoman competing against entire teams.

The night before the combined AAU Nationals and U.S. Olympic Trials held on July 16, 1932, at Northwestern University, Didrikson was too nervous to sleep. The following day, when the competing track teams were introduced at the opening ceremonies, she stepped out onto the field by herself. Feeding on the enthusiasm of five thousand amazed fans, she rushed from event to event—eight in all. The heat was so stifling that some athletes brought hundred-pound blocks of ice and sat on them to keep cool between events.

Didrikson, however, seemed unaffected by the conditions. She set world records in the 80-meter hurdles and javelin, and tied with Jean Shiley for a world record in the high jump. She also finished first in the shot put, long jump, and baseball throw, and took fourth in the discus. When the team results were announced, Didrikson stepped forward to claim the trophy. She had single-handedly collected 30 points, to finish well ahead of the second-place Illinois Women's Athletic Club, which garnered 22 points. The magazine *Amateur Athlete* wrote, "Is it necessary to say that Miss Didrikson expects to win all of the individual track and field events for women in the Olympic Games at Los Angeles?"[25]

On to the Olympics

Unfortunately for Didrikson, Olympic officials proved to be tougher obstacles than her competitors. Although she had qualified for the Olympics in six events at Northwestern, officials would not budge from their rules that prohibited a woman from competing in more than three events. Didrikson reluctantly settled for the three in which she had set world records.

As she headed to Los Angeles, Didrikson was idolized by the nation. The press admired her ability and her feisty confidence, calling her the "Texas Tornado." When asked who she thought would give her the most competition at the Olympics, she replied, "I don't know who my opponents are and, anyway, it wouldn't make any difference. I hope they are good."[26] Such statements led one reporter to write, "The Texas girl is all fight from the tip of her toes to the top of her straight black hair."[27]

However, while the press eagerly followed the story of her success, they were not fond of her personality. Didrikson did not act like most women they knew. She seldom bothered to comb her hair, much less dress nicely or put on makeup.

As always, Didrikson managed to irritate and offend her team-mates. Her habits—such as chewing tobacco, constantly working out in the aisle of the train taking the women athletes to Los Angeles, and incessantly playing the harmonica—did not endear her to the other women, nor did her cold-blooded obsession with winning. Her seventeen-year-old roommate in Los Angeles, sprinter Mary Carew, remembered that although Babe was kind to her, "she bragged all the time. She wasn't liked by the other girls because nobody likes a bragger, but she didn't care."[28]

High jumper Jean Shiley agreed that while Didrikson had a fun sense of humor, she was not a good sport. "I think a lot of girls found her behavior a little beyond how they thought a young lady should act," said Shiley. "Nobody did anything better than she did. I don't care if it was swallowing goldfish; she would have to swallow more goldfish than anyone else."[29]

The Javelin

More than sixty thousand fans packed the Los Angeles Coliseum on the Sunday afternoon that Didrikson was to compete in the javelin throw, in which women were competing for the first time at the Olympics. At the start of the competition, one of the officials placed a German flag on the ground to mark the official

Babe Didrikson set the world record for the javelin throw at the 1932 Olympics in Los Angeles.

world record. Didrikson was unimpressed; she had thrown the twenty-six-ounce spear well beyond that mark many times.

During her warm-ups, her muscles had felt tight. Before she was able to get them completely stretched out, it was time for her first throw. The tightness forced her to throw in a slightly awkward manner, and the javelin slipped out of her hand. As she described it, "Instead of arching the way it usually did, that javelin went out there like a catcher's peg from home plate to second base. It looked like it was going to go right through the flag. But it kept on about 14 feet past it."[30]

The crowd thundered its approval as the world-record distance was announced: 143 feet 4 inches (43.7 meters). Unfortunately, Didrikson was unable to provide any more thrills for the home crowd. Unknown to her, she had torn cartilage in her right shoulder on the throw. The injury prevented her from uncorking an even better throw. Didrikson could only stand by helplessly as Germans Ellen Braumüller and Tilly Fleischer zeroed in on her mark. Braumüller's best throw landed very close to the mark for Didrikson's first toss.

Didrikson (left) crossed the finish line inches ahead of Evelyn Hall to win the gold medal in the 80-meter hurdles.

The Americans breathed a sigh of relief as the throw measured just six inches short of Babe's throw, and Didrikson walked off with her first gold medal.

Hurdles

On Wednesday, another huge crowd came out to cheer on the record-setting Texan as she ran the 80-meter high hurdles. Didrikson's main rival in this event was another American, Evelyn Hall, of Chicago. Both women won their qualifying heats, setting up a closely anticipated final race.

The crushed peat track in the Coliseum felt light and springy to the runners. So eager was Didrikson to shatter another world record on the fast track that she jumped the gun at the start. Olympic racers are allowed one false start; a second automatically disqualifies them. Unwilling to risk the humiliation of disqualification, Didrikson had to sit back in the starting blocks instead of leaning forward in anticipation. As a result, she got off to a slow start, well behind Violet Webb of Great Britain. Evelyn Hall's start was no better than Babe's.

The race proved to be a contest between Didrikson's speed and determination and Hall's flawless hurdling technique. Didrikson would pull just ahead of Hall between the hurdles only to have Hall pull even on the jump. As they came off the final hurdle, they appeared to be dead even, with Hall surging from the momentum of her smooth leap. Didrikson put on a furious final burst, and the two flashed across the finish line almost in unison.

While the timers and judges discussed the result, spectators debated which of the women had won. Some were convinced that Hall had won, based on the fact that she had a welt on her neck that apparently came from the finishing tape. The evidence of photographs and the reports of timers and judges, however, indicated that Didrikson crossed the finish line just inches ahead of Hall. As she expected, her winning time of 11.7 seconds was another world record.

High Jump

Controversy over the hurdles results had barely quieted before an even greater controversy marred Didrikson's last event, the high jump. Here, she faced a formidable opponent in Jean Shiley.

Shiley was a physical education major at Temple University in Philadelphia, who many considered to have been the world's premiere high jumper over the previous four years. As a sixteen-year-old, she had won at the U.S. Nationals and had gone on to finish fourth at the 1928 Olympics in Amsterdam. In the recent U.S. Olympic Trials, she had tied with Didrikson for first place with a world-record leap of 5 feet 4-1/4 inches.

At this time, the rules on high jumping for women were strict. The jumper had to take off with one foot and land on the other, and the head and shoulders could not go over the bar before the rest of the body (this was considered "diving"). Shiley's scissors-style technique conformed exactly to the rules, while Didrikson's homemade form skirted the edge of legality. Since Babe rolled over the bar, the way the top male jumpers did, instead of scissoring it, there was some question whether she was diving. Didrikson admitted that she had to execute the jump perfectly in order to prevent it from being a dive.

The Olympic judges appeared to have no problem with Didrikson's technique. Shiley and Didrikson battled furiously, with neither giving an inch. Both soared over their previous world record and kept going. Both cleared 5 feet 5-¼ inches. Finally, the two rivals missed at 5 feet 6 inches.

The judges declared a jump-off to break the tie. The bar was set back at 5 feet 5-¼ inches, which was still higher than any woman had ever jumped before. Shiley cleared the bar. Didrikson matched her.

At this point, the officials stepped in. They disqualified Didrikson for diving and awarded the gold medal to Shiley. Didrikson was furious, claiming that she had jumped no differently this time than she had all day or at any time during the Olympic Trials. Shiley agreed with her, except in her view, Didrikson had been diving all day. "Babe was not jumping according to the rules," said Shiley. "There really should have been no controversy at all. I don't know why it took the judges until our jump-off to decide that Babe was jumping illegally."[31]

Didrikson's only consolation was that the controversy eventually forced Olympic officials to abandon the restrictive rules and give women the freedom to jump as the men did.

More Controversy

Didrikson probably would have gone on to collect many more gold medals and world records had she not gotten into yet another controversy. A few months after achieving celebrity status as the star of the 1932 Olympics, Didrikson allowed an automobile dealer to use her name, photograph, and a personal interview in an advertisement. Although she claimed she had not intended the photo and interview to be used in this way, it was a violation of the eligibility rules for both track and field and the Olympics. On December 5, 1932, the AAU declared, "By sanctioning the use of her name to advertise, recommend, and promote the sale of an au-

Capitalizing on her Olympic fame, Didrikson appeared in exhibition games with major league baseball teams.

tomobile, Mildred (Babe) Didrikson had automatically disqualified herself for further participation as an amateur."[32]

With track and the Olympics no longer part of her life, Didrikson worked quickly to capitalize on the fame her efforts had brought her. She went on tours around the country playing exhibition games in both basketball and baseball. A couple of major league baseball teams even gave her a chance to match her skills against pro ballplayers. Although pitching was one of the weakest of all her athletic skills, she hurled two scoreless innings for the Cleveland Indians in an exhibition game against a minor league team. She also pitched an inning for the St. Louis Cardinals in an exhibition versus the Philadelphia A's.

In 1934 Didrikson tired of these entertainment spectacles and settled into a new sport—professional golf. Now known as Babe Didrikson Zaharias following her marriage to professional wrestler George Zaharias, she totally dominated the sport for two decades. During the 1940s, she won seventeen tournaments in a row, and she was instrumental in forming the Ladies Professional Golf Association in 1950.

Didrikson developed cancer in 1953 and underwent an emergency colostomy. Still tough as rawhide, Babe was back on the golf tour within three months. In 1954 she completed her comeback by winning the U.S. Women's Open, blowing away the field by twelve strokes. The cancer returned, however, causing her death on September 17, 1956, at the young age of forty-five.

Legacy

Babe Didrikson was arguably the most celebrated female athlete of all time. Six times in her career, she won the Associated Press's Award as the Woman Athlete of the Year (1931, 1945–47, 1950, 1954) and was honored as the AP's Female Athlete of the Half Century.

Her many athletic accomplishments are all the more remarkable in that she was neither a large woman (5 feet 5 inches, 105 pounds in her prime), nor did she have the benefit of excellent coaching. Her track-and-field skills were primarily self-taught, a fact attributed to her stubbornness as much as anything else. Olympic coaches tried to help her improve her javelin, hurdling, and high-jumping form, but she refused to listen to them. Most of what she accomplished came from sheer athletic skill and fiery determination.

Didrikson's undeniable athletic ability and fierce competitiveness gave the women's Olympic movement a huge boost just at the time when it was reeling from criticism that women were not suited for competitive sports. She also opened the eyes of Americans to the possibility of women playing any sport, even those traditionally reserved for men, and playing it well. According to Olympic historian Allen Guttman, "No other person in the history of women's sports, with the possible exception of Billie Jean King, has had the influence of Babe Didrikson."[33]

CHAPTER 4

Fanny Blankers-Koen

Babe Didrikson's domination of sports in the 1930s produced an unfortunate side effect for female athletes. According to analyst Adrianne Blue, Didrikson was "the first athlete to make people confront issues of femininity; how much muscle is too much? How much is unfeminine?"[34] Didrikson's hard-as-nails nature and her disdain for traditionally feminine behavior fueled the prejudices of those who thought women did not belong in athletics. If a woman had to act and look like a man to succeed at sports, they said, what was the point of encouraging her to participate? To them, Didrikson was an exceptionally masculine woman who simply provided more proof that competitive sports, like war, were masculine activities.

Although Sonja Henie had proven that a very feminine woman could succeed at athletics, the critics dismissed her as more of an entertainer than an athlete. It was not until the arrival of Fanny Blankers-Koen that female athletes began to overcome their unfair reputation as male wanna-bes. Blankers-Koen was a quiet wife and mother of two children who also happened to be one of the most spectacular female athletes in track-and-field history.

Fanny Blankers-Koen at home with her husband and two children.

Jesse Owens's Autograph

Francina Elsje Blankers was born on April 26, 1918, in Baarn, the Netherlands. Like Sonja Henie, she came from a family that encouraged her to take part in athletics. At the age of six, she joined a local sports club in Amsterdam, where she enjoyed skating and tennis.

World War II interrupted the Olympics for twelve years and postponed Blankers's Olympic goals.

Eventually, she took up competitive swimming with the goal of reaching the Olympics. "I've made up my mind to go in for sport,"[35] she announced to her family. Although she won her share of early meets, one of her coaches advised her to switch sports. The Netherlands was filled with fine young female swimmers, she was told. But the nation was weak when it came to track and field. So, at the age of sixteen, Fanny shifted her efforts to the sport at which her father, a shot-putter and discus thrower, had excelled.

Success did not come immediately to the tall blond runner. She finished far back in her first race for the Amsterdam Dames Athletic Club, a 200-meter dash in 1935. But a month later Blankers defeated the Dutch champion in the 800 meters. Among those who viewed the upset was Jan Koen, a coach for the Dutch track-and-field team going to the 1936 Berlin Olympics. At his urging, the seventeen-year-old was immediately asked to join the team. Her biggest problem was determining which event she should focus on. Blankers seemed equally good at both short and long sprints, hurdles, and jumping events.

For the 1936 Olympics, Blankers concentrated on the high jump and running the second leg of the 4 x 100-meter relay. She was nervous about competing against the world's top athletes before so many thousands at the Berlin stadium. She did well for a young, inexperienced competitor, finishing in a tie for sixth in the high jump and helping her relay team to a fifth-place finish. But she was content to enjoy the experience and remain just another face in the crowd. For her, the highlight of the Games was getting the autograph of U.S. sprint star Jesse Owens.

Interruption

Following the Olympics, Fanny improved with every race she ran. By the end of 1937, she had become the Netherlands' top sprinter. In 1938 she placed third at the European Championships in Vienna, Austria. As the 1940 Olympics approached, the Dutch had high hopes that Blankers could capture a gold medal in at least one of her events.

Unfortunately, Adolf Hitler's German army roared through Poland just five months before the Olympics were to take place. Whereas the ancient Greeks suspended their wars in order to hold the Olympics, the modern nations did just the opposite. The 1940 Games were canceled.

Fanny shrugged off the disappointment. She married her coach, Jan Koen, in August of that year, but they were able to enjoy only a few months of quiet contentment before the Nazis overran the Netherlands. Fanny's track-and-field career seemed effectively ended. Although she continued to train during the German occupation of the Netherlands, no international track meets were held while the war raged. Fanny had to content herself with winning national titles and setting world records in the high jump and long jump.

The Athletic Mother

It appeared as though Fanny would never get the opportunity to demonstrate her talents to the world. At about the time the war finally ended in 1945, she became pregnant with her second child. No one imagined that a mother of two could compete in track and field at a world-class level. Most doubted it was physically possible for her to regain her speed even if her duties as a mother were not too time-consuming for her to train.

Blankers-Koen, however, was not ready to give up the sport she loved. She did not see any reason why she could not be a good mother and continue to train hard. Squeezing in workouts when she could, she regained enough of her former speed that, just seven months after giving birth, she entered two events in the 1946 European Championships in Oslo. Although she was still far from peak condition, she managed to win the 80-meter hurdles and anchor the Dutch team to victory in the 4 x 100-meter relay. After years of suffering under the Nazi occupation, the Dutch took special pride in her success.

Blankers-Koen came to believe that even though she was well past the age when most women retire from sprinting, she could not only regain her former skill but could actually improve on it. Every day she rode her bike to the track with her two children sitting in a basket strapped over the rear wheel. While the children played in the sand of the long-jump pit, their mother worked out under the direction of their father.

Her efforts paid off spectacularly. In the late 1940s, Blankers-Koen set new world records in the 100-meter dash, the 80-meter hurdles, the high jump, and long jump, and anchored two world-record relay teams.

But not everyone applauded her efforts. Many people were outraged that a married woman would spend her time on sports and that she would expose her legs at public track meets. According to them, she ought to be focusing on caring for her family. "I got very

Fanny Blankers-Koen won the gold medal in the 80-meter hurdles, one of the four she would eventually win at the 1948 Olympics.

many bad letters," said Blankers-Koen, reflecting on those times. "People writing that I must stay home, that I should not be allowed to run on a track in short trousers."[36]

Instead of answering questions about Fanny's training schedule, Jan Koen found himself having to defend her fitness as a wife and mother. "My wife is a real housewife," he told the press. "She cooks, cleans, and takes care of our children. She sews and knits their clothes."[37]

The Olympics at Last

When the Olympics resumed in London in August 1948 after a twelve-year break caused by World War II, Fanny found even more criticism awaiting her. Despite the evidence of her world records, the British press refused to believe that a thirty-year-old mother could stand up to the pressure of Olympic competition. They predicted that she would be unable to hold off the challenges of the younger competitors.

Despite the negative press, Fanny was ready to dominate the Games as they had never been dominated before. Unfortunately, although the rules limiting women's participation had been relaxed somewhat, she ran into the same problem that had thwarted Didrikson. She could not compete in all the events in which she excelled. She decided to skip the jumping events and concentrate on races.

Her first race was the 100-meter dash. Fanny immediately quieted her critics by posting the fastest time of the preliminaries—12.0 seconds. As she crouched at the starting line for the finals, she fought hard to control her nerves. Her chance for a gold medal had finally come. But in twelve long years of anticipating this moment, never in her worst dreams had she imagined such a miserable setting for an Olympic race. A heavy rain had been falling for days at Wembley Stadium. She stared down at a cinder track that had been turned into a sea of mud between her and the finish line. Shrugging off the conditions, Blankers-Koen took off at the crack of the gun and steadily opened a small gap on the field. Kicking up mud behind her, she hit the finish tape a full three meters ahead of her nearest rival. Due to the sloppy track, her time of 11.9 seconds was well off her world record of 11.5, but she was pleased just to have finally won her medal.

"God Save the King"

Unlike the 100 meters, which Fanny won without a serious challenge, the 80-meter hurdles promised to provide stiff competition. Maureen Gardner, a nineteen-year-old ballet instructor from Great Britain, had posted times close to Fanny's world record and had been steadily improving. Battling her own case of nerves, Gardner hit a hurdle so hard in a preliminary heat that she stumbled badly and barely qualified for the finals. Nevertheless, Blankers-Koen, who had qualified easily, expected a close battle.

As the gun went off, Gardner flew out of the starting blocks, leaving Blankers-Koen behind. Desperately, Fanny raced after her, narrowing the gap with each hurdle. By the time she reached the final barrier, Blankers-Koen caught her rival and appeared ready to blow past her to the finish tape. But she was going so fast that her steps were slightly off and she banged the last hurdle. Fighting to keep her feet, she lurched awkwardly to the finish line, with Gardner next to her, leaning for the tape.

The tremendous duel had pushed each to their fastest times, despite the soft track. Timers caught both at 11.2 seconds, a tenth of a second better than the world record. But in a scene mirroring the confusion of the Didrikson-Hall hurdle race, the officials conferred for several minutes in an attempt to determine who had won.

Suddenly, a band began to play "God Save the King," the national anthem of Gardner's country. Blankers-Koen slumped in disappointment, believing she had lost. The band, however, was simply responding to the entrance of King George and Queen Elizabeth at the stadium. After much discussion, Blankers-Koen was declared the winner.

"You're Too Old"

While the Dutch fans joyfully celebrated Blankers-Koen's accomplishments, Fanny did not share their feelings. Always jumpy before any competition, she found the attention showered on her at the Olympics terrifying. "Far from exuberant about these accomplishments," writes sports historian David Wallechinsky, "she felt tremendous pressure to win a third gold medal and was close to a nervous breakdown."[38]

It did not help matters that she had to try for the third gold medal in what appeared to be her weakest race. The 200-meter dash was the only one of her events in which she did not hold the world record. Before her semifinal heat, Fanny told her husband that she could not go on. Jan tried to settle her down, but Fanny kept asking to be withdrawn from the race. Fearing that his wife was letting the opportunity of a lifetime slip away, Jan pleaded with her to run the race for the memory of his parents and for her small children. The speech worked. After breaking into tears, Fanny agreed to stay in the competition. She won her heat easily and advanced to the finals.

Concerned that Fanny might have a relapse of nerves, Jan tried to keep her competitive fires stoked. Just before she walked out onto the track, he winked at her and said, "Remember, Fanny, you're too old."[39] He need not have worried. By this time, the tall blond sprinter was eager to go after her place in history.

The 200-meter race was no contest. Blankers-Koen glided away from the competition in the first fifty meters. As the crowd whipped into a frenzy, she kept increasing her lead, as though she somehow had the only dry land and the rest were mired in the mud. She crossed the finish line to a huge roar of approval, nearly seven meters ahead of the silver medalist. Although the soupy track slowed her time to 24.4 seconds, short of the world-record mark, she captured her record-setting third gold medal with the largest margin of victory in the history of the 200-meter race.

What Could Have Been

Now that the pressure of winning the three golds was off, Blankers-Koen was able to relax and enjoy her final event—the 4 x 100-meter relay. Her three teammates in the event ran hard, but they had nowhere near Fanny's ability. The Dutch team dropped back from the leaders until it seemed impossible that even Blankers-Koen could make up the difference. When her teammate handed the baton off to her on the final curve of the track, the Dutch team was in fourth place, and all the teams ahead of them had saved their best runners for last.

Blankers-Koen rocketed down the track. She pulled into third and then eased by the second-place team. Australian sprinter Joyce King, however, appeared to be out of reach. "The Flying Dutch Housewife," as the press had begun calling Fanny, put on a final burst of speed. In a nail-biting finish, she caught the Australian and hit the tape in a time of 47.5, just one-tenth of a second ahead of King. She had earned a fourth gold medal to add to her collection.

Blankers-Koen finishes the 400-meter relay.

Blankers-Koen, standing behind her young son, was honored for her Olympic achievements by both the Dutch government and the entire nation.

The most amazing part of Blankers-Koen's record-setting Olympic performance is that she did not even take part in what many considered her best event. Prior to the Olympics, Fanny had posted a long jump of 20 feet 6-¼ inches. She was so far ahead of her competition in that event that this would stand as a world record for more than four years. There is little doubt that Blankers-Koen could have sailed far past the gold-medal-winning performance of 18 feet 8-¼ inches by Olga Gyarmati.

Had Fanny been able to take part in the high jump, she likely could have added another gold medal. She was the reigning world-record holder in this event as well, and the winning jump of Alice Coachman of the United States was an inch and a quarter short of Blankers-Koen's record of 5 feet 7-¼ inches.

The Grand Old Lady of Track and Field

When Blankers-Koen returned home from the Olympics, she found that she had become a national heroine. The Dutch government gave her the nation's highest honor by naming a variety of rose after her. A candy manufacturer named a candy bar after her. Her hometown of Amsterdam gave parades in her honor, and her neighbors gave her a bicycle, joking that the present was "so she won't have to run so much."[40]

Although she appreciated the gifts, the shy Blankers-Koen was uncomfortable with the fuss being made over her. She never tried to capitalize on her medals or her fame. She continued to train and race when she was nearly twice the age of many of her competitors. In 1950 she dominated the European Championships, winning the same four events she had won in the London Olympics. In 1952 she again qualified for the Olympics, held in Helsinki, Finland, that year. Although thirty-four years old and battling a string of injuries, she managed to equal the Olympic record in the 80-meter hurdles in a qualifying heat. In the finals, however, her Olympic winning streak came to an end. Blankers-Koen hit the first two hurdles, which threw her so off-stride that she had to drop out of the race.

She continued to sprint until 1956, when, at the age of thirty-eight, she still managed to post a world-class time of 11.3 seconds in the 100-meter dash. That year she finally decided to hang up her spikes. She retired to a quiet life with her family, although residents of Amsterdam often saw Fanny riding around the city on the bike her neighbors had given her.

Legacy

No woman track-and-field performer has ever enjoyed a career as long lasting and wide ranging as that of Fanny Blankers-Koen. Although best known for winning four gold medals in a single Olympics, she also won fifty-eight Dutch National Championships, competed internationally for eighteen years, and set thirteen world records in a total of six different events. Had the Olympics not been derailed due to World War II, she likely would have collected more gold medals than any other woman in Olympic history.

In addition to her outstanding records, Blankers-Koen helped revitalize women's athletics by counteracting the stereotype of female athletes as male impersonators. For all that she did to demonstrate what a woman could accomplish in athletics, Babe Didrikson appeared to be something of a special case. She was a unique personality, who seemed totally uninterested in anything traditionally feminine.

In contrast to the brash, combative, tobacco-spitting Didrikson, Blankers-Koen struck many as a fascinating blend of feminine and athletic qualities. IOC president Avery Brundage, who had disparaged Babe Didrikson, hailed Blankers-Koen as "a new type of woman—lithe, supple, physically disciplined, strong, slender, and efficient, like the Goddesses of ancient Greece."[41] Women's sports advocates pointed to her as a role model who showed that sports were for all girls, not just for tomboys.

Some of the praise of her as a role model was unfair and stereotypical. When Blankers-Koen was thrilling the crowds at the 1948 Olympics, newspapers often focused more on her home life than on her athletic achievements. "Fastest Woman in World Is an Expert Cook,"[42] is one example of the headlines plastered on sports pages, as if this was proof to uncomfortable sports fans that Fanny was a real woman who knew her place in society.

But in the long quest for access to athletics, prejudicial stereotypes had to be overcome one at a time. By proving that a gentle mother of two children could enjoy and excel at athletics, Fanny Blankers-Koen showed a skeptical world that athletics did not destroy traditional feminine qualities. In doing so, she opened up the world of sports to a much wider range of women.

CHAPTER 5

Dawn Fraser

Dawn Fraser complained to reporters that if only officials would let her swim naked she could break every record in the books. Although societal attitudes had changed a great deal from the days when a woman showing any skin other than her face and hands was considered scandalous, it was still an outrageous comment for a woman to make in the 1960s.

Fraser liked to say what was on her mind even if it caused a stir; in fact, there were those who suspected she liked to say what was on her mind *because* it caused a stir. During her competitive career, she was almost constantly in trouble with swimming officials upset with her behavior.

The Australian swim star seemed to thrive on the outrageous and the unusual. From her family background to her training style to her lifestyle, Fraser was unlike any other swimmer of her time. Following the flight of her own free spirit, she rose above all her rivals and stayed on top for three consecutive Olympics.

Australian swimmer Dawn Fraser thrived on doing things in outrageous and unusual ways.

"Get Yourself to the Top"

Dawn Fraser was born on September 4, 1937, the youngest of eight children born to a working-class family in Balmain, an industrial suburb of Sydney, Australia. Her father was a soccer player who had visited Australia while touring with the Scottish national team and had decided to settle there. He worked for meager pay on a ship, and both he and Dawn's mother were often in poor health. This left the family scrambling to make ends meet. Dawn spent much of her spare time as a child staying home and taking care of the house when her parents were incapacitated.

Dawn learned to swim at the age of five when her older brother Don took her to a Sydney pool. But, unlike most of Olympic competitors, she did not begin competing until much later. Her parents never prodded her; in fact, while her father was a devoted fan of many sports, he had no interest in swimming. Dawn swam purely for fun and to keep cool.

It was a battle-of-the-sexes dare that coaxed her into the sport. Once while she was at the pool, she crossed paths with some boys at a swim team practice. She said later, "I hated the easy assumption that girls had to be slower than boys."[43] The brash Fraser told the boys she could beat all of them. The boys' swim coach, Harry Gallagher, invited her to put up or shut up. Dawn accepted that challenge. As she kept pace with the boys, Gallagher recognized her natural talent and invited her to train with him.

Again, Dawn received no encouragement from her parents. It was her brothers, all of whom played soccer, who persuaded her to accept Gallagher's offer and give competitive swimming a try. Dawn's mother gave her blessing, on one condition. "If you want to swim, you go get yourself to the top,"[44] she told her.

Socks on the Starting Block

Championship swimmers tend to start early and burn out quickly. The fourteen-year-old Fraser started out her career racing against girls who were five- and six-year veterans and were already nearing their peak performances. Many of them were pressured by their parents into competing. Fraser felt sorry for them, and relieved that her own parents were not watching over her shoulder. "I've always believed that the desire must come from within,"[45] she said.

The pressure of competing against more-experienced racers sometimes overwhelmed her. At a meet in Sydney, Fraser anxiously began peeling off her warm-up suit before her race when an official hurriedly stopped her. She had been so nervous about the race that she had forgotten to put a swimsuit on underneath her sweats! On another occasion, she crouched at the starting line

Before Dawn Fraser, no Australian swimmer had won a medal since Mina Wylie (left) and Fanny Durack's impressive 1912 performances.

waiting for the starting signal when she realized that she still had on her socks.

But she quickly showed a strong, fluid swimming motion and a strong work ethic. At 5 feet 8-1/2 inches and 149 pounds, Fraser had plenty of strength for an overpowering final kick. In addition, she had the advantage of a good coach, whose workouts she followed to the letter. The work paid off and Fraser's times dropped dramatically.

For several years, however, Fraser saw little of the world other than churning water and the tiles of swimming pools. She competed in no international meets prior to entering the 1956 Olympics.

Olympic Dream

After the impressive performances of Fanny Durack and Mina Wylie back in 1912, the Australians had surrendered domination of the swimming events to the United States and northern Europe. No Australian had won a gold medal in the intervening years.

In 1956, however, the Australians burst into the forefront of women's swimming. Dawn Fraser led the charge. On February 21, she broke the world record in the 100-meter freestyle, a mark that had been held by Willy den Ouden of the Netherlands for twenty years. Displaying the typical brashness that would later get her into trouble, Fraser commented to reporters that she had not swum all that well and could certainly do better.

Fraser's teammate Lorraine Crapp could have said the same thing. Over the next eight months, she waged a seesaw battle with Fraser for bragging rights for the 100 meters. The two of them broke the world record six times while tuning up for the Olympics. As the Games began, Crapp again held the mark at 1 minute, 2.4 seconds (1:02.4), more than three seconds faster than the standing Olympic record.

In the first heat of the preliminary rounds, Crapp set the pace and grabbed the Olympic record with a swim of 1:03.4. A few minutes later, Fraser skimmed through the water in 1:02.4. Both swimmers held back a little in the semifinals, Fraser clocking a 1:03.0 heat, while Crapp cruised in at 1:03.1 to set up the decisive battle in the finals.

Fraser tried to calm her jumpy nerves before the first important race of her life. She went to bed early and lay there thinking through every stroke of the race, particularly the turns. Eventually, she fi-

Fellow Australian Lorraine Crapp (pictured) was Fraser's closest competitor in the 1956 Olympics.

nally drifted off to sleep, where she experienced a terrible nightmare. She was standing on her starting block at the pool, poised for the crack of the gun. When the shot went off, she found her feet were slathered so thickly with honey that she could barely pry them off the block. When she hit the water, she found it full of spaghetti. She thrashed and thrashed but found herself barely moving.

After suffering through such a horrible dream experience, Fraser found the real event almost peaceful by comparison. She exploded off the starting blocks with Crapp a fraction of a second behind. The two had barely hit the water when they began pulling away from the competition. Swimming smoothly, Fraser hit the turn first. Inch by inch, Crapp narrowed the gap until, with twenty-five meters to go, they were dead even. Both swimmers fought with every last ounce of energy, and when they hit the wall, most spectators were uncertain who had won. The judges awarded the victory to Fraser in a world-record time of 1:02.0. Crapp, earning the silver medal, had also beaten the former mark, with 1:02.3. Adding to the stunning Australian triumph was the bronze-medal finish of their teammate Faith Leech. Fraser accepted her medal tearfully, thinking of her brother Don, who had introduced her to this sport and had since died.

The Australian stars waged another battle in the 400-meter freestyle, which was Crapp's best event. This time the world-record holder held off Fraser, who had to be content with the silver medal. The two stars then joined forces in the 4 x 100-meter relay. With Fraser swimming first and getting the team off to a comfortable lead, Australia easily won the gold.

Defending Her Crown

During the next four years, many of Fraser's competitors retired. But the late-starting Dawn, who had been the oldest of the Australian women swimmers at the 1956 Games, felt as though she was just getting started. When the routine of swimming began to feel a little stale, Fraser sought out a different challenge by taking up a new event—the butterfly. Before long, she was swimming world-class times in that event.

As the 1960 Olympics approached, Fraser was almost forgotten in the hype over Australia's newest swim stars, John Konrads and his sister Ilsa. Although John was only seventeen and Ilsa fifteen, each had claimed six world records in swimming. In March 1960, swim fans crowded around an outdoor pool to see the wonderkids perform in a meet. Fraser watched from the shadows in amusement. This was just the sort of challenge she needed to motivate her.

As she and Ilsa approached the starting blocks for the 440-meter freestyle, Fraser let her young rival know that she was not intimidated. "Anyone for a swim?"[46] she joked. Then in the race, she bided her time for seven laps, content to let Konrads set the pace. On the final lap, she unleashed a devastating kick and stormed past Konrads to win the race.

In that same meet, Fraser churned to a world record in her new event, the 100-meter butterfly. Forty-five minutes after touching the wall in that race, she swam against Konrads again, in the 100-meter freestyle. Despite swimming in a driving rain, Fraser trimmed 1.2 seconds off her own world record of 1:01.4. Fraser then capped her incredible performance by shattering the world record for the 200-meter freestyle with a time of 2:11.0. That was the last time Konrads, or any other Australian, threatened to dethrone the reigning swim champ.

The Pillow Fight

American swimmer Christine von Saltza provided some stiff competition for Fraser at the 1960 Olympics in Rome. During a qualifying round, she broke Dawn's Olympic record with a time of 1:01.9. Fraser immediately won back the record in her heat with a time of 1:01.4, and then cruised to victory in the finals with a time of 1:01.2. That made her the first woman to successfully defend an Olympic swim title.

Fraser ran into more trouble outside the pool than in it, in preparations for a new Olympic event, the 4 x 100-meter medley relay. In this race, each of four team members would swim a different stroke: backstroke, breaststroke, butterfly, and freestyle. The night before the event, Fraser had stayed out late celebrating her gold-medal victory. She explained, "I knew the 400 medley relay was on that day, but I had been told I wasn't to swim on our team."[47]

At a team meeting the morning of the race, there was a violent argument. According to varying press reports, Fraser either slapped one of the other swimmers or smacked her in the face with a pillow. Fraser's version is that three of the younger girls on the team were swearing at the coach. She thought it was inappropriate and threw a pillow at them to get them to stop.

Fraser then went out for a morning of shopping and sightseeing in Rome. Believing that she was not scheduled to swim, she ate a large spaghetti lunch. Just as she was finishing, a coach came to tell her that she would be swimming the butterfly leg of the medley relay. Having stuffed herself with pasta, Fraser said she was not prepared to swim and refused. Another teammate resolved the

Dawn Fraser (left) is seen with Ilsa Konrads in 1958 congratulating John Konrads after one of his record-breaking victories.

problem by volunteering to swim for her. But Dawn's teammates bitterly resented both her refusal to swim and her actions at the team meeting. For the rest of the Olympics, none of them spoke to her. Australian officials later suspended Fraser for her behavior.

Love of Swimming

While most swimming experts expected, and some hoped, that Fraser would soon burn out in this demanding sport, the tireless Australian kept going. Relentlessly, she kept at her grueling training routine that included workouts in both the morning and afternoon. She began with warm-up laps during which Coach Gallagher looked for, but seldom found, any flaws in her form. During the morning, she worked on sprints and on her turning technique. In the afternoon, she strove for endurance with sixteen fifty-five-meter sprints, followed by sixteen more using only her legs. Then she would finish with a half-mile swim at a slower pace. Were it not for her love of swimming, there was no compelling reason for her to continue. All of Fraser's fame and success brought her next to nothing in the way of financial rewards. During her Olympic career, she lived in a small apartment and supported herself on low-paying jobs such as a salesclerk in a department store and a public relations director for a recreational center.

Fraser was able to last so long as a competitive swimmer because of her unique personality. She saw no reason why she had to dedicate every moment of her life to the pool. Dancing was her first love, and she went out three or four times a week, often staying out late. If she happened to stay out too late and did not feel like swimming the next day, she simply skipped the workout.

"I probably have a different mental approach to swimming than most people," she explained.

> I actually enjoy training most of the time. When I don't want to train, I don't. If it comes, it comes, and I don't force myself. Nine years ago when I started to swim seriously, I did everything my coach, Harry Gallagher, told me to, but then two years ago I began using my own judgment more and more, and we both feel the arrangement is better.[48]

Fraser also looked for ways to have fun in the pool. She enjoyed the fact that the tables were turned from the days in the pool when she would taunt and challenge the boys. Once she became a star, boys frequently tried to prove they could get the best of her. Fraser calmly sped past them as she completed her workout.

"Granny" Fraser

Throughout the early 1960s, Fraser showed no signs of slowing down. On October 27, 1962, she became the first woman to break

Fraser with silver medalist Sharon Stouder (left) and bronze medalist Kathleen Ellis (right) after winning the gold in the 100-meter freestyle at the 1964 Olympics.

the one-minute barrier in the 100 meters. Two years later she swam the distance in 58.9 seconds, a record that would last eight years.

One month after that outstanding performance, Fraser was driving a car that skidded out of control and crashed into a parked truck. Her mother was killed, and Fraser had to spend six weeks with her neck in a plaster cast because of chipped vertebrae. Even that tragedy, however, did not stop the tireless swimmer. Seven months later, she was back in the 1964 Olympic finals of the 100-meter freestyle.

This time, Sharon Stouder of the United States took dead aim at the champion. Although Fraser broke out to an early lead, Stouder caught her with thirty meters to go. It seemed as though momentum was on the side of the American. With an incredible show of willpower, Fraser found an extra burst and slipped past Stouder for her third straight gold medal in that event. On much more pleasant terms with her teammates this time, she then anchored the Australian 4 x 100-meter freestyle relay team to a silver medal.

For those who wondered how long the woman whom her teammates called "Granny" could keep going, Fraser slyly hinted that she was not through yet. "It wouldn't be impossible, you know, to win a swim medal at 30,"[49] she said, anticipating the 1968 Olympics when she would be that age.

Typically, however, the free-spirited swimmer found herself embroiled in more Olympic fusses. First, she broke team rules by marching in the opening parade when the coaches had ordered her to rest up for her races. Then, she had refused to swim in the team's regulation suit, arguing that it was too restrictive. Finally, on a whim, she decided to sneak out of the Tokyo Olympic village at night and raid the Imperial Palace. She climbed a fence, swam across a moat, and came away with a "souvenir" flag. The authorities were not amused by the prank and Fraser was arrested.

Although the charges were dropped and the emperor gave her the flag as a gift, the Australian Swimming Union was not as forgiving. At about the time Fraser was honored as Australian of the year, the Union slapped a ten-year suspension on her. The suspension was eventually lifted after four years, but by then it was too late. After such a long layoff, even Dawn Fraser could not think of reviving a swimming career at her age. She had long since retired from the sport. The suspension did nothing to diminish her popularity among Australians, however. In 1990 Fraser was elected to the Australian parliament.

Legacy

Dawn Fraser blazed a path that carried a long line of talented Australian women to world prominence in swimming. Few athletes in any sport have dominated a single event for as long as she ruled the 100-meter freestyle. She held the world record for the event for fifteen years and made Olympic history by being the only woman ever to win the same event in three consecutive Olympics. In addition, she was a major force in helping Australia to four relay medals.

Along with her record of success, Fraser showed that women swimmers did not have to be robots who start at an early age, endure a joyless career of workouts, and then burn out young. While she may not have always exercised the best judgment, Fraser showed that a world-class woman athlete could have fun and did not have to relinquish her unique personality.

CHAPTER 6

Lydia Skoblikova

None of the athletes in this book has enjoyed the Olympic success of Lydia Skoblikova. Yet at the same time, few people have ever heard of her. A reader can thumb through dozens of accounts of Olympic history without finding more than a brief sentence or two about the woman who was arguably the greatest female Olympic athlete of all time.

Skoblikova had the misfortune of being caught in the cross-fire of the Cold War between the United States and its Western European allies and the Soviet Union and its Eastern European allies. Rather than a friendly competition designed to bring people of all nations together, the Olympics in the late 1950s and 1960s degenerated into a political and propaganda battle-ground. Soviet athletes such as Skoblikova were given very limited coverage in the Western press. As the enemy, they could hardly be portrayed positively even if Westerners had any interest in them.

Furthermore, Skoblikova had to live in the shadow of suspicion that surrounded both the Soviets and East German women as they vaulted to the top of the sports world. Were they professional athletes in violation of Olympic rules that allowed only amateurs? Were they on performance-enhancing drugs? Were they women at all? As a result, few appreciated Skoblikova for the astonishing athlete that she was.

The Schoolteacher

Lydia was born on March 8, 1939, in Zlatoust, deep in the heart of Siberia. Her father worked as a metallurgy engineer in this small mining town in the mountains. Even when living in one of the coldest places on earth, Lydia did not like to be cooped up indoors throughout the long winter. She learned to cope with the elements by participating in such outdoor sports as skating. She showed such promise at this sport that, at the age of twelve, she decided to dedicate herself to serious competition.

In 1957 the eighteen-year-old Lydia married her trainer, Alexander Skoblikova. As Lydia improved into one of the Soviet Union's top speed skaters, Alexander passed her on to other coaches and became a teacher at the Chelyabinsk Pedagogical Institute, also in Siberia. Noting that most of her teammates were married to skaters, Lydia was glad that her husband had found other work. "I think it's better not to be married to a skater," she once told reporters. "You have more to talk about."[50]

Lydia Skoblikova prepares for one of her many speed skating competitions.

The Soviet Sports System

Lydia was a bright woman with a passion for a wide range of subjects, including literature and music. She focused her professional career on the teaching of anatomy in Chelyabinsk. As she developed into a world-class speed skater, she received financial support from the Soviet government and was given plenty of time off to train.

The reason for this was that during the 1950s, the Soviet Union targeted the Olympics as a way to improve the morale of their people and demonstrate the superiority of their Communist form of government. They undertook an ambitious program to promote sports, including offering government subsidies to successful athletes so they could concentrate on their events without having to work at other jobs. The Soviets officially denied the existence of such subsidies, which were a violation of the Olympic rules requiring athletes to be amateurs competing solely for the love of the sport.

The Soviet government made it clear that its aims were not the camaraderie and friendly competition espoused by the Olympics. "All athletes competing in foreign countries are especially trained and are taught to compete in a fighting spirit," the official government policy stated. "Competitions are not just sporting events. They carry a tremendous ideological and political charge; they demonstrate the aspirations of the Soviet people."[51]

A New Olympic Event

Women's speed skating appeared to be especially fertile ground for this political demonstration. For many years, the sport was a victim of the old Olympic taboos against women competing in strenuous events. The 1960 Winter Olympics at Squaw Valley, California, were the first to include it on the program. Rather than simply dip their toe in the waters, the organizers authorized four races, including the grueling 3,000 meters (just under two miles). Since there was no established power in women's speed skating, the events were ripe for conquest by the Soviet sports establishment.

The Soviet skaters at Squaw Valley were well steeped in the philosophy of patriotic domination. As one of Skoblikova's teammates, Maria Isakova, remarked, "As I raced around the ice I never forgot for a moment I was representing Soviet sports and carrying its banner."[52]

The most outstanding of the Soviet skaters at Squaw Valley was Skoblikova. The speedster from Siberia entered three of the four events, passing on only the shortest sprint—the 500 meters. Lydia sped to a razor-thin victory over Poland's Elvira Seroczynska in the 1500-meter race, capturing the first gold medal in Olympic women's speed-skating history. In the 1,000 meters, she skated well but finished fourth, just missing a bronze medal in an event won by her teammate Klara Guseva. It was the last time anyone would beat Skoblikova in Olympic competition for many years.

In speed skating, the competitors race in pairs to avoid congestion on the ice. Since their main competitors often are not on the track with them, they are forced to race against the clock. This involves a lot of waiting and watching the scoreboard for competitors' times. In the 3,000 meters, Skoblikova knew she would face tough competition from teammate Valentina Stenina. But none of the other skaters could match her time of 5:14.3, and so she collected the second of her gold medals.

Intrasquad Competition

The intensely competitive Skoblikova enjoyed her triumphs but felt that the Olympics left some unfinished business concerning the 500 meters. She did not want to leave the impression that she was slower than the German winner, Helga Haase, or the other Soviets who had been chosen to represent her country. At the speed-skating World Championships later that year, she entered the 500 meters and claimed first place in that event as well.

Having made her point, Lydia dropped out of international competition for a couple of years and spent more time teaching school. But with the Olympics coming up again in 1964, she swung back into action in 1963.

The training routine for the Soviet women skaters was both innovative and exhausting. Long before in-line skates became a marketable product, the Soviets developed a type of skate with four thin rollers in a line to use during the months when ice was not available. They found that the technique used with these skates, especially in turns, was identical to that of ice skates. Coach Elena Stepanyenko claimed that the roller skates were actually better than ice skates because they were heavier and built up the leg muscles more quickly.

The skaters began their workout with a ten-minute warm-up, followed by twenty minutes of jumping, bending, stretching, and flipping to increase their flexibility. The next quarter hour was spent simulating the skating motion, without skates—raising the legs high and kicking backward. After skating some 200-meter sprints, the women spent twenty minutes jumping forward from a skating crouch. Then, according to the skaters, the real work began, most often in the form of a long series of 200-meter dashes broken up by brief intervals of rest.

The U.S. and Soviet delegations enter the ice arena in Squaw Valley, California, at the beginning of the 1960 Winter Olympics.

The Soviet women were friendly but fierce rivals. They were all aware that they were the best skaters in the world, all competing furiously for the same spots in the Olympics. But none could match Skoblikova's intense will to win. "I enjoy being the strongest in the world," she told reporters. "At the theater, you applaud a good actor who gives you pleasure. When I have won a race, giving people pleasure, I like to skate around the stadium, wearing the laurel wreath of victory."[53]

In order to achieve those glorious moments, Lydia was willing to work as hard as she had to. "If anyone else runs 20 times 200 meters, I can do 40 times 200," she claimed. "And at a faster speed."[54]

Gender Issues

The sudden dominance of the Soviet women in many sports led to suspicions that they were cheating in ways other than financial support. Rumors and whisperings followed some of their star athletes whose appearances were undeniably masculine. Were they really women or men posing as women to help boost the Soviet medal count?

The glare of suspicion shone most brightly on the Press sisters from Leningrad. Tamara Press was a huge, powerful athlete who annihilated all of her competition in both the shot put and discus. Irina Press, while not as hulking, was a better athlete who specialized in the five-event women's pentathlon. Between them they set twenty-six world records and won five Olympic gold medals in the 1960s.

Their suspicious physiques led to the initiation of sex testing to determine whether all competitors in international sports were really women. No sooner were these tests initiated than the Press sisters abruptly retired.

During this time, it was Lydia Skoblikova who shielded her Soviet sisters from the blanket accusations of the embittered foes they de-

Tamara Press's physique and her record-breaking shot-put throws fueled rumors that she was really a man.

feated. No one even thought of suggesting that the 5 foot 5 inch, 126-pound Soviet blond, whom reporters invariably described as attractive, was a female impersonator. Skoblikova was outspoken in defending her teammates against sneers that competitive sports made women too masculine. "Skating makes us more feminine,"[55] she declared. As if to prove her point, Skoblikova designed her own costumes, including her favorite black one that accented the female figure.

The Surest Bet

Competition on the Soviet team was so stiff that even a defending double–gold medal winner had trouble holding her place as the team's ace skater. During Skoblikova's absence from competition, Inga Voronina erased almost all of her world records, leaving her with only the 1,000-meter mark. Voronina, however, developed a stomach ailment so severe that it required hospitalization. Her recovery was painfully slow and left the field wide open for Skoblikova. At the 1963 World Championships in Karuizawa, Japan, Lydia could not break Voronina's records, but she did perform the astounding feat of winning all four speed-skating events.

Skoblikova seemed unimpressed with her accomplishment. "The others were just skating worse than I was,"[56] she said with a shrug.

The rest of the world took a different view. In a preview of the 1964 Winter Olympics to be held in Innsbruck, Austria, *Sports Illustrated* noted, "The surest bet of the Olympics is that Lydia Skoblikova, the attractive 24-year-old Russian speed skater . . . will win a gold meal. . . . [S]he might win four if the Russians let her enter that many races."[57]

As in 1960, the debate was whether or not Skoblikova should race in the 500 meters, which remained her weakest event. Although Voronina was still recovering from her illness and unable to make the team, the Soviets were loaded with world-class skaters such as Valentina Stenina, Tatyana Sidorova, Irina Yegorova, and Klara Nesterova. The Russian coaches debated whether to risk overloading their star with four tough races when so many capable racers were on hand to ensure victory. In the end, they decided to let Skoblikova try for a historic sweep of all the events.

The great skater had second thoughts of her own about entering all the races. The Soviet team was so powerful that she was certain that several of her teammates had a good chance at a gold medal in the 500 meters if she did not enter. She worried that she would appear greedy because she would be depriving a teammate of what might be her only chance to win a medal. Lydia's husband ended her indecision, however, by sending a simple telegram. "Win just as many gold medals as you can,"[58] he urged.

The Weakest Race

The weather was unusually warm in Innsbruck during the Olympics. The ice on the skating track was occasionally slushy, and sometimes covered with a thin film of water that made footing treacherous. This caused great anxiety for many of the skaters, but Skoblikova ignored the conditions and concentrated on keeping her form.

For her, the first race would be the toughest. The Olympic schedule called for the 500-meter race to lead off the speed-skating competition. Soviet skater Irina Yegorova was first on the track. Despite a slow track from the melting ice, she blazed around the circuit in a time of 45.4 seconds, beating the Olympic record by half a second. Her teammate Tatyana Sidorova skated an almost identical race, and crossed the finish line a mere tenth of a second behind Yegorova's time, also well ahead of the Olympic mark.

Luck of the draw had put Skoblikova in the thirteenth of the fourteen skating pairs. As she waited for her turn, watching the scoreboard carefully, the ice continued to melt. Lydia charged furiously from the starting line. She leaned so far forward as she skated that her upper body was almost parallel to the ice, a position that she held even in the corners. This technique required exceptional balance. At one point Skoblikova slipped on the wet ice but managed to stay on her feet. Recovering quickly from the near disaster, she accelerated through the final turn and shot through the final straightaway to the finish. The clock flashed 45.0 seconds, giving her the gold medal.

Skoblikova broke into tears of relief at having claimed victory in her weakest race. Her teammates swarmed around her, showering her with praise and affection. "Now cut out that kissing," she complained. "I can't get any air."[59]

No Surprises

Having seen Skoblikova so easily dispose of the opposition in the sprint, skating experts fully expected Skoblikova to win the next three races. The only thing that might stop her was possible exhaustion from shouldering the pressure of being an Olympic favorite for so many races.

But if the pressure bothered her, none of the spectators could see it. The day after her 500-meter triumph, Skoblikova took advantage of cooler weather and a harder track to rocket around the course in the 1500-meter race. Her time of 2:22.6 was almost three seconds ahead of second-place Kaija Mustonen of Finland.

Day three of the speed-skating competition offered nothing in the way of surprises. Lydia blazed to her third Olympic record in three races. Her winning time of 1:33.2 in the 1,000 meters was a comfortable 1.1 seconds ahead of her silver-medalist teammate Yegorova. Now the only question was, did she have enough stamina left after three days of intense competition to last through the exhausting 3,000 meters?

Perfect Ice

If the sloppy ice caused problems in the sprint races, it was even more of a concern in the long-distance event. A slow track meant

Lydia Skoblikova completes the 1500-meter race. Skoblikova won the gold medal in the event at the 1964 Winter Olympics.

Skoblikova overcame poor skating conditions to win the 3000-meter race and capture her fourth gold medal of the 1964 Winter Olympics.

the skaters would have less glide and would have to work even harder to keep up their speed. Soviet coaches wondered if Lydia had enough strength in reserve after the other races to overcome this obstacle.

Once again, though, Skoblikova refused to worry about conditions. On the eve of her attempt to become the first woman to win four individual gold medals in an Olympics, she slept soundly. The Soviet ace was so relaxed, in fact, that she arrived at the stadium late. She had to quickly lace up her skates and rush through a warm-up.

Skating in the seventh pair, she tried to stay on an Olympic record pace. The ice, however, was not cooperating. In some spots, Skoblikova was skating through puddles. As a result, her splits (the times called out at the end of each lap) were not nearly as fast as she had hoped. "My morale fell when they called it to me," she explained later. "Then I speeded up and they called to me to slow down for fear I would fall."[60]

"Take it easy," her coaches shouted. "Don't hurry your steps."[61]

Although reluctant to give up on her quest for a record time, Skoblikova took the coaches' advice. She crossed the finish line in 5:14.9, well ahead of teammate Valentina Stenina's 5:18.5. Lydia and her supporters had to survive a few anxious moments when the last skater, Han Pil-hwa of North Korea, matched Skoblikova's pace for four-and-a-half laps. The tiny unknown skater finally wore down, however, and finished in a tie with Stenina for the silver medal.

In winning her fourth gold medal, Skoblikova was typically gracious. She eased the embarrassment of her Austrian hosts over the slushy ice by insisting that the ice had been perfect.

Legacy

Lydia Skoblikova attempted to give an encore in the 1968 Winter Olympics in Grenoble, France. But by then she was on the downside of her career and unable to recapture the magic. Although she actually improved her time in the 3,000 meters on a fast track to 5:08.0, she had to settle for sixth. She placed a disappointing eleventh in the 1500 meters.

By then, however, her place in Olympic history had been etched in stone. Skoblikova's record of four individual gold medals in one Olympics, and her total of six individual golds in two Olympics, are marks that have never been equaled.

The Siberian speedster also advanced the cause of women's athletics in two ways. First, she was a key member of a Soviet national women's team that pushed the limits of achievement far beyond those of the previous generation. In 1964 she was the first woman honored as the Soviet Athlete of the Year. The Russians' success in turn pushed East Germany, the United States, and other countries into developing female athletes. Many U.S. sports fans who had previously scoffed at women's sports came to support their nation's athletes out of patriotic pride in competition against their Cold War enemy.

Second, Skoblikova stood out as an important contradiction to the stereotype of Soviet female athletes as cold, masculine machines. Her combination of incredible strength and endurance, grace under pressure, willingness to let her emotions show, and pride in her appearance reinforced the idea that women could be warm and feminine and still enjoy and excel in sports.

CHAPTER 7

Nadia Comaneci

A tiny bundle of muscle whirled around the uneven parallel bars with blinding speed. Even those among the sixteen thousand spectators crammed in the Montreal Forum and those watching on television who were not familiar with gymnastics held their breath as a 4 foot 11 inch, 86-pound girl from Romania risked her neck in one dangerous move after another. Nadia Comaneci drew gasps as she let go of a bar, spun through the air, and regrabbed the bar. As she finished her routine, landing steady and straight as an arrow after her dismount, the crowd broke into deafening applause.

Nadia Comaneci's score of a perfect 10 was the first in the history of the modern Olympic Games.

The judges faced an awkward moment. Occasionally in Olympic competition, gymnasts had performed so well that the judges had awarded 9.9 out of a possible 10.0 points. In a few rare instances, gymnasts had executed a difficult routine so flawlessly that they had received a 9.95. This performance on the uneven parallel bars, however, had topped anything the judges had ever seen. One observer called it "biomechanically inconceivable."[62] What score could they give her? In Olympic gymnastics scoring, it had long been a standing tradition that no one could achieve a 10.0. After all, no one was perfect, and even if someone appeared to give a flawless performance, what would the judges do if someone came along who did even better?

The Playground Discovery

The utterly fearless young lady who caused this dilemma was born on November 12, 1961, in Onesti, Moldavia, a region of Romania. Nadia Comaneci's father, Gheorghe, was an auto mechanic in this mining town of forty thousand near the Carpathian Mountains. Her mother, Alexandrina, worked as a hospital caretaker. The standard of living in Onesti was not high, and both parents struggled to provide the basic necessities of life for Nadia and her older brother.

Nadia was an unusually serious child, but she was also active and loved to perform acrobatic tricks. When she was in kindergarten, Bela Karolyi and his wife visited Nadia's school. Karolyi was a gymnastics coach at a sports school, and he was scouting for young children with gymnastics potential. As Karolyi watched the children run and jump on the playground, Nadia immediately caught his eye with her agility and coordination.

Before he could find out her name, though, a bell rang and the children ran into the school. Karolyi chased after Nadia but lost sight of her as the children hurried into their classrooms. He had not even gotten close enough to get a good look at her. Determined to track down the young prospect, the coach visited one classroom after another.

"Who loves gymnastics?"[63] he asked, hoping to draw out the mystery girl. Finally, in one of the classes, Nadia jumped up eagerly at the question. Karolyi recognized her as the one he was after, found out who she was, and approached her parents about enrolling her in the sports school. Young athletes were privileged in Romania. Those accepted into Karolyi's National Institute of Gymnastics received education and coaching paid for by the Romanian government. Even meals and lodging were provided free of charge. Given such an offer, the Comanecis readily agreed, and six-year-old Nadia embarked on a gymnastics career.

Controversial Coach

Comaneci worked out under the guidance of a man who would become perhaps the most controversial coach in the history of gymnastics. Bela Karolyi was a tough, unforgiving man who demanded perfection even from his youngest students. "We are not in the gym to be having fun," he repeatedly told his students. "The fun comes in the end with the winning of the medals."[64] Even as a beginner, Comaneci practiced eight hours a day, seven days a week. In contrast, she spent only two hours a day in the classroom.

Karolyi refused to accept any excuse for failure, not even injury, saying, "With or without injury they have to compete, and they must compete without any kind of doubt."[65]

To many observers, Karolyi's methods flirted with the line between tough leadership and child abuse. He especially came under fire for an obsession with weight. Heavier gymnasts could not fly around as nimbly as thin ones, and he constantly was after the girls to lose weight. Some of his students reported that when they did not maintain the weight he wanted, he denied them food.

Because of his harsh, demanding coaching style, Bela Karolyi has been the subject of much controversy.

Comaneci, however, was a tough, determined child who responded well to the rigorous training. Shrugging off sympathy over the demanding training schedule and Karolyi's harsh methods, she said, "I come from a very poor family. If this work is hard, what about my parents?"[66]

Comaneci insisted that her coach "loves his gymnasts as much as he loves his own kids."[67] She maintained this defense even though Karolyi could be as hard on her as on anyone else. When Nadia competed in her first Romanian National Junior Championships at the age of seven, she finished thirteenth. Karolyi responded by buying her a doll. The doll was not a reward, however, but a stern reminder. Every time she looked at the doll, it would remind her of her poor finish and inspire her never to place so poorly again.

Unique Student

While Comaneci did not always develop as quickly as Karolyi wished, he soon realized that he had found a unique student. There were six characteristics that put Nadia ahead of the others, he said. Three of them were physical traits: strength, speed, and agility. Nadia had been blessed with natural ability in all those areas and, through hard work, was building on those skills.

The three mental characteristics that Karolyi cited were harder to develop: courage, intelligence, and concentration. The young Comaneci was utterly fearless when it came to trying new and dangerous tricks. Karolyi found that his young student would not flinch at trying moves that not even the world's best gymnasts would attempt. Comaneci was also a quick study who caught on right away to what was taught to her.

Perhaps her most unusual gift was the ability to completely block out any distractions while she was performing. Her somber face rarely changed expression no matter what the level of competition. Even with critical judges watching her every move in a gymnasium packed with screaming spectators, Nadia seemed totally unaware that anyone else was in the room.

Armed with these skills, Comaneci began improving at a startling rate. Responding positively to Karolyi's harsh doll present, the eight-year-old returned to the Romanian National Junior Championships in 1970 and won the all-around title. Three years later, she was ready for her first international junior competition, which she also won.

A Child Against the World's Best

For the next couple of years, Comaneci chomped at the bit, waiting until she turned old enough to compete at the senior level against the best gymnasts in the world. In January 1975, she finally was eligible for this final rung of competition. She entered a small meet in January and came away with the gold medal in the all-around competition.

Two months later, Comaneci faced a challenge that she had been dreaming about for years. Her coach entered her in the European Championships at Skein, Norway, where she would have to compete against the Soviet Union's trio of superstar gymnasts: Lyudmila Tourischeva, Olga Korbut, and Nelli Kim. Tourischeva, the graceful and elegant defending Olympic champion and five-time European Champion, had been Comaneci's idol for many years. Korbut, a tiny package of explosive energy with an infectious grin, had captured the hearts of gymnastics fans throughout the world. And Kim, the Soviets' latest star, exhibited a combination of Tourischeva's style and Korbut's athleticism.

Such a lineup would have intimidated any inexperienced gymnast, not to mention one who was only thirteen years old. But once Comaneci stepped onto the mat, all other cares disappeared from her world. From her first routine, the young Romanian put on a show that dazzled her older Russian rivals.

There are four separate exercises in women's gymnastics. There is the balance beam, in which competitors perform their moves on a slab of wood four inches wide; the uneven parallel bars, in which gymnasts whirl back and forth between two bars, one of which is higher than the other; the vault, which is a running, tumbling jump over a vaulting horse; and floor exercise, in which competitors perform routines with tumbling and dancing on a large mat. Individual medals are awarded in each event, but the most prestigious prize is the all-around championship, which is a combination of the scores in all four events.

Comaneci not only held her own against the stiff competition; she outshone everyone. On the first day, she won the all-around championship. She added individual event victories in the vault, uneven bars, and balance beam the next day and finished second to Kim in the floor exercise.

The World Is Watching

Nadia's performance made her an instant star in Europe. Yet she entered the 1976 Montreal Olympics as only a slight favorite over

This multiple exposure photograph shows the grace and agility exhibited by Nadia Comaneci on her way to winning a gold medal in the balance beam.

the Russian trio, who had been stung by Comaneci's triumph and had trained furiously to recapture their edge. Most North Americans tuning in to the Olympics had never heard of the Romanian.

Comaneci arrived at the Olympics totally unaware of the massive exposure that ABC television had planned for her. The network had spent a fortune on broadcast rights to the Olympics and was searching for a star who would attract a massive audience. They decided to place their bets on the fourteen-year-old. As one network executive said, "We figured Comaneci would be big for us. People maybe were discovering her for the first time but we've been working her into *Wide World of Sports* [a weekly sports television show] for a year or more now."[68]

The first day of gymnastics was the team competition, pitting the underdog Comaneci and Romania's team, the youngest Olympic gymnastics team ever, against the powerful and experienced Russians. Preliminary hype over the barely teenaged sensation attracted capacity crowds to every gymnastics session at the Montreal Forum. Curious television viewers tuned in to see what the fuss was all about.

Oblivious to the glare of her newfound celebrity status, Comaneci exceeded ABC's wildest expectations. She started off on the balance beam, where millions of viewers got their first look at the poker-faced young lady with the elastic body and nerves of steel. The four inches of beam seemed as wide as a sidewalk the way she jumped and somersaulted and flipped along its length. The judges rewarded her with a sparkling 9.9 score.

Perfection

While Comaneci scored well in all events that day, she saved the best for last. The setting could not have been more dramatic. All other competitors had completed their first-round routines. As Nadia chalked up her hands for her turn on the uneven bars that could lift the Romanians into the lead over the Russians, all eyes were on her.

With all that pressure on her, Comaneci did not even flinch. Even the experts were awestruck by the flawless blur of motion as Nadia wrapped herself around the bars. In the words of one, "She stunned the judges not only with double somersaults and twists, but also with an uncommon consistency and stability even in her most difficult moves. . . . [S]he had classical style with its emphasis on maturity and ladylike grace."[69] Comaneci finished off her exercise with a twisting dismount far more difficult than anything anyone had ever tried in competition.

Comaneci awaits the results of her performance at the 1976 Olympics.

Olympic officials were caught unprepared for such a performance. Although Comaneci had scored perfect 10s in some of her previous competitions, no one expected it would happen in the Olympics. Never in the eighty-year history of the Olympics had a 10 been awarded on this most prestigious stage. Most judges could not imagine a circumstance under which they would give it.

When her score finally appeared on the board, Comaneci's heart nearly stopped. She thought she had done so well, and yet her score was listed as a disastrous 1.00! But it was quickly apparent that the scoreboard designers had been as unprepared as everyone else for Comaneci's performance. The scoreboard was not designed to display a score of 10.0 and this was the best it could do.

Star of the Olympics

That magic moment guaranteed that Comaneci would be the star of the Olympics. For the rest of the week, millions of television viewers watched her battle against the Russians. The young Romanian did not disappoint. Proving that her feat of cracking the unthinkable perfect-ten barrier was no fluke, she went on to record six more 10s, including perfect scores in all her routines on the uneven bars.

Despite her flawless efforts, the Romanians fell just short of their goal of defeating the Soviet Union for the team title. Co-

Nadia Comaneci with her parents, Gheorghe and Alexandrina.

maneci, however, mined plenty of gold in Montreal. She captured first place in the all-around competition, the uneven bars (in which she put together back-to-back scores of 10.0), and the balance beam (where she recorded a 10.0 and a 9.95). In addition, her lively floor exercise, accompanied by the popular American tune "Yessir, That's My Baby," earned her a bronze medal. Comaneci narrowly missed medaling in all the events when she placed fourth in the vault.

Comaneci proved to be as oblivious about the significance of her performance as she was to the distractions of the arena. She considered her success a simple matter. "I knew that if I worked hard I would win,"[70] she told reporters. When the press gushed to her that she had done gymnastics moves never attempted in competition before, she shrugged and said, "I like to do things nobody else does."[71]

In later years, Comaneci admitted that her nonchalance was no act; that she was actually too overwhelmed by the experience to understand its significance. "I got to travel," she said. "If you ask if I realized what I did then, I had no clue."[72]

In fact, for Nadia, performing seemingly impossible gymnastics moves was easy compared to the dreaded press conferences. Comaneci was no more prepared than any other fourteen-year-old to field a barrage of questions from relentless reporters. When asked by one to reveal her greatest wish, she answered, "I want to go home."[73]

Struggles

Although Comaneci was hailed as a national heroine in Romania, her fame did not prevent her life from falling into a tailspin of turmoil. When Coach Karolyi was removed from the Romanian national team, Nadia gained weight and lost her training focus. At one point, she faked drinking bleach in an attempt to pressure the government to reinstate him.

In 1980 the government relented and Karolyi came back. Comaneci went to Moscow with him to defend her Olympic titles. This time, she found herself in a tight duel with the Soviet Union's newest star, eighteen-year-old Yelena Davydova, for the all-around title. As the competition wound down, Comaneci found herself in another pressure-packed situation. If she scored a 9.95 on the balance beam, she would win the gold; a 9.9 would give her a tie.

Since Comaneci had received a 9.9 and a 10.0 on her previous beam routines, she appeared to be in good shape for victory. Performing in awestruck silence, she executed another unique and incredibly difficult exercise. Experts noted one tiny flaw in one of her twisting forward flips. Nonetheless, many observers expected she had done well enough to at least share the title.

The judges conferred for nearly half an hour before awarding her a 9.85, thanks to a Soviet judge who awarded her a 9.8 and preserved victory for the home country. Nadia did walk away with first place in the individual balance beam and a gold medal for tying Nelli Kim in the floor exercise, which had been her weakest event in Montreal.

Burned out at last by the grueling years of training, Comaneci retired before the 1984 Olympics. For the rest of the decade, she kept a low profile, working as a gymnastics coach. As the years went on, she grew disenchanted with the depressing economic conditions in her home country. On November 27, 1989, she made the difficult choice to leave her family, her medals, and her apartment and defect to the West. She walked six hours in the darkness through mud and ice to reach the Hungarian border. Eventually, she reached the U.S. embassy in Vienna, Austria, and was granted permission to live in the United States.

Legacy

Nadia Comaneci will be remembered as the unflappable girl who achieved a level of perfection once thought impossible. Her daring and demanding routines accelerated the trend in gymnastics from emphasis on subtle, artistic grace to a more physically demanding, acrobatic sport. She also raised the expectations for every gymnast who followed her. Comaneci pioneered the technique of release moves on the uneven bars, spinning and whirling through the air. It was Nadia who introduced triple back handsprings on the balance beam and a twisting back somersault dismount off bars—a move known as the Salto Comaneci in her honor.

By performing her breathtaking moves so flawlessly before a huge curious television audience, Comaneci helped propel a women's sport into the most widely watched of all Olympic events. Unfortunately, her success also spurred a trend that many health and sports experts found disturbing. The tiny fourteen-year-old was the youngest person ever to win an Olympic gold medal in gymnastics. After watching her performance, gymnastics coaches immediately turned their focus on young undersized girls like her. On the U.S. Olympic team, for example, the average female gymnast who competed against

Comaneci stands among U.S. and Romanian gymnasts in August 1999.

Comaneci was 17-$\frac{1}{2}$ years old, 5 feet 3-$\frac{1}{2}$ inches tall, and weighed 106 pounds. By 1992 the average gymnast on the U.S. Olympic team was 16, 4 feet 9 inches tall, and weighed a mere 83 pounds.

As one critic explains, "It is far easier to work with small, mute creatures who look at a coach as an idol and perform everything without talking back."[74] For most young athletes the incredible stress of high-stakes gymnastics is unhealthy and even dangerous. Comaneci was able to excel in such a situation because she was an exceptional athlete who seemed immune to pressure.

CHAPTER 8

Jackie Joyner-Kersee

Jackie Joyner got involved with track and field simply because she could not stand to be left out of anything. She wrote her name down on every sign-up sheet that was passed around her neighborhood recreation center. The track team sheet just happened to be one of them.

After several days of running around a track, all of the other girls who had signed up decided it was too much work. Jackie did not like to quit; but when the only runners left were Jackie and her two younger sisters, whom she forced to come with her, the rec center disbanded the track team.

Unwilling to give up, Jackie joined a rival elementary school's track team. In her first race with this team, she finished dead last. After finishing last or near last in every race that summer, even her cheerful dedication began to fade. "Am I ever going to win anything?"[75] she wondered.

She could never have imagined at that time that one day she would be standing on an Olympic platform listening to the national anthem with a gold medal dangling from her neck.

Tough Childhood

Jacqueline Joyner was born on March 3, 1962, in East St. Louis, Illinois, to Al and Mary Ruth Joyner. Her parents named her after the nation's first lady, Jacqueline Kennedy, at her grandmother's insistence. "Someday this girl will be the First Lady of something,"[76] Ollie Mae Johnson said proudly.

For a long time, that seemed like an empty prophecy. Jackie lived with her parents, brother, and two sisters with her grandmother in a house that one writer describes as "little more than wallpaper and sticks."[77] Her father had been laid off his job on the assembly line of an aircraft manufacturer. Eventually he found work in Springfield, a hundred miles away, and Jackie's mother got a job as a nurse's assistant, but money was always tight. The furnace often broke down, causing the water pipes to freeze and burst, and sending Jackie to sleep in the kitchen next to the stove. Although she loved school, Jackie was embarrassed to have to go in worn-out, secondhand clothes, with mayonnaise sandwiches for lunch.

The East St. Louis neighborhood deteriorated and became overrun with drugs, gangs, and criminals. Shootings and murders took place within sight of the family's house. Jackie's older brother Al said of their childhood, "I remember Jackie and me crying together in a back room in that house, swearing that we were going to make it. Make it out."[78]

From Dance to Track

The two saving graces in Jackie's life were a disciplined but loving family and the newly constructed Mary E. Brown Community

Jackie Joyner and her brother Al celebrate a victory during the 1984 Olympics in Los Angeles.

Center. "All the kids from the neighborhood spent time at the Center," she remembers, "but I practically lived there."[79] She tried virtually every sport and craft the community center offered, but her favorite activity was dance. When her instructor told her that she had the talent and long legs to go far in dance, she dreamed of pursuing a career on Broadway. That ended when her teacher was shot to death, and the classes were discontinued.

Joyner began running track at the age of nine. While trailing far behind other competitors in the races, she cast envious eyes over at the long-jump pit. She had always loved jumping. She and her sisters took potato chip bags to nearby Lincoln Park and filled them with sand from the playground to make a sandpile in their front yard. Then Jackie would practice leaping out into the pit from the porch.

Her coach had never imagined the slow-footed girl could do well at long jumping, and Jackie never pushed the issue. But one day while she was waiting for a ride home from the coach, she took a try at the long-jump pit. Her coach happened to arrive just

Young Jackie Joyner was determined to match the athletic success achieved by Olympic gold medalist Wilma Rudolph (pictured).

as her long legs stretched far out into the sand. "Do that again!"[80] he said, hardly able to believe the distance she had achieved.

High School Star

As Joyner grew, her long legs began to carry her past opponents in races as well as in the long jump. When she was fourteen, she goaded her sixteen-year-old brother Al into a race and beat him. The humiliation persuaded Al to join the track team to get in better shape. He eventually developed into an Olympic gold-medal winner in the triple jump.

Meanwhile, Jackie was finding motivation of her own in Olympic role models. At first she patterned herself after U.S. sprint star Wilma Rudolph, who had won three gold medals in 1960. Joyner made up her mind to do everything she could to match her success. Along with her teammates, she worked tirelessly at car washes, bake sales, and door-to-door solicitation to raise money so their team could attend important track meets.

Jackie was so driven to succeed that she would not even allow herself a momentary lapse of effort. "Once during a track practice," she remembers, "we were running a long route around the neighborhood. We stopped off for a snack at a friend's house and then took a shortcut back to school so the coach wouldn't know we hadn't run the full course. Later, I felt so bad that I went out and ran the course in the dark."[81]

With that kind of determination, Joyner blossomed into an athlete who dominated every sport she tried. Although she did not start playing basketball until her sophomore year at Lincoln High School, she was named an All-American by the end of her junior year and led her team to the Illinois state title her senior year. She was an All-Metro selection in volleyball. But it was in track and field that Joyner really shone. Along with winning state titles in the 400-meter dash and the long jump, Jackie won four consecutive National Junior Championships in the pentathlon—the five-event track-and-field contest that tested a woman's all-around athletic ability.

Growing Up Fast

In her senior year, Jackie set an Illinois state record of 20 feet 7-$\frac{1}{2}$ inches in the long jump. That earned her an invitation to compete in the 1980 U.S. Olympic Trials. She held up well against the pressure of facing world-class athletes for the first time, recording a personal

Jackie Joyner attended UCLA on a basketball scholarship, but was also still able to compete in track-and-field events.

best of 20 feet 9-³/₄ inches. But even that left her in eighth place and off the Olympic team. She realized she still had a lot of work to do.

Jackie, who had ranked thirteenth in her class academically, moved on to attend the University of California at Los Angeles

(UCLA) on a basketball scholarship. She made the coaches promise, however, that she could also compete in track and field for the school. While trying to juggle a difficult class load and two major sports, she found the underpinnings of her life falling apart. First, she and her mother broke off relations with her increasingly abusive father. Then, with no warning, her mother developed a severe case of meningitis and died during Jackie's freshman year. Meanwhile, the UCLA track coaches looked at her as a basketball player who was only competing in the long jump for fun. They gave her little coaching, and Jackie began to struggle.

During this difficult period, Joyner caught the attention of a young assistant coach named Bob Kersee. Although hired to coach sprinters and hurdlers, he recognized Joyner's untapped potential and gave her individual coaching in track-and-field techniques.

Under Kersee's guidance, Joyner improved her all-around skill enough to win the NCAA heptathlon title in 1982, with a record 6,088 points. (The more demanding heptathlon had recently replaced the pentathlon in women's track and field. It consists of seven events: the 100-meter hurdles, high jump, shot put, 200-meter dash, long jump, javelin, and 800-meter run.)

In the winter of 1983–84, Joyner took a leave of absence from the basketball team to focus on the Olympics. After working out for eight hours a day, she qualified for the Olympic heptathlon team with a national record in the heptathlon of 6,520 points. Joyner also made the team in the long jump.

Mental Lapse

Originally, Joyner had set a goal of winning the bronze medal at the 1984 Los Angeles Olympics. But when many of the strongest athletes, particularly the East Germans, decided to boycott the games, she began to think about gold.

Her optimism ended two weeks before her event when she strained a hamstring muscle in practice. Instead of focusing on caring for the injury, Jackie stewed and moped about her misfortune. Although Kersee encouraged her to be aggressive, she held back in the hurdles and high jump for fear of aggravating the injury. Nonetheless, she finished the first day in second place, ahead of her strongest competitor, Austria's Glynis Nunn. With her best event, the long jump, leading off the next day's competition, Joyner appeared to be in great shape.

Jackie, however, could not shake the worry over her leg. Losing her concentration, she fouled on her first two jumps. That forced her to play it safe on her last attempt, and her jump was more than two feet off her best mark. The poor effort finally ignited her competitive fires. She performed well in the javelin and entered the final event, the 800 meters, with a slight edge over Nunn. This was not Joyner's strongest event, but she knew she had to stay within two seconds of Nunn to take the gold medal. With her brother Al coming over from the triple-jump competition to scream encouragement at her, Jackie tried to keep her rubbery legs and knotted arms going. But she crossed the finish line an agonizing .33 seconds short of victory.

Jackie knew that she had lost out on the gold because she had not been mentally tough. She vowed that would never happen again.

The 7,000-Point Barrier

Following the 1984 Olympics, Joyner went back to playing basketball and studying. She ended her basketball career at UCLA among the top ten in school history in points, rebounds, and assists. At the same time she maintained a B average working for a degree in communications and history.

But her main love was track and field, which also happened to be Bobby Kersee's life. The two began spending more and more time together and eventually married in January 1986. But the coach could not resist including a motivational needle in the bargain: Jackie could not take his last name until she broke a world record.

Joyner accepted the challenge, and it was not long before she listed her name as Jackie Joyner-Kersee. At the Goodwill Games in Moscow on July 7, 1986, she not only broke the world heptathlon record, but became the only woman to break the 7,000-point barrier.

Unlike most heptathletes, Joyner-Kersee never seemed to hit a plateau. She kept improving in all events until she was the undisputed queen of the event. During the four years between the Olympics, she won every heptathlon competition she entered. As the 1988 Olympic Games in Seoul, South Korea, approached, the only drama was over how high Jackie could push the record.

The Wrong Leg

Joyner-Kersee showed she was serious about a record when she led off the 1988 Olympic heptathlon competition with a personal best time of 12.69 seconds in the 100-meter hurdles. The injury-prone star, however, hurt her knee in the high jump and had to settle for 6 feet 1-¹/₂ inches—2-¹/₂ inches below her best.

At Los Angeles, such an injury had wrecked her concentration. This time Jackie shrugged it off. She went over to the shot-put circle and tossed the iron ball 51 feet 10 inches for another personal best. The competition was virtually over by the end of the first day when Jackie blazed to the finish line in 22.56 seconds in the 200 meters, a full second and a half faster than she had run in 1984.

Her injured knee began acting up again as she warmed up for the long jump on day two of the heptathlon competition. So confident was Jackie of victory that she deliberately jumped off the wrong foot to avoid stress on the knee! The adjustment did not hurt her score a bit. She managed a distance of 7.27 meters (23 feet 10-¹/₄ inches), an Olympic record for the long jump.

Joyner-Kersee then uncorked one of her best javelin throws ever (45.66 meters), and finished the 800 meters nearly five seconds faster than her 1984 time. That gave her the unbelievable total of

Jackie Joyner-Kersee (right) set an Olympic record in the 100-meter hurdle event of the heptathlon at the 1988 Olympics.

7,291 points. To put this in perspective, Sabine John and Anke Behmer of East Germany, the silver and bronze medalists, both topped the previous Olympic record. Yet neither was ever close to contending for the gold medal, which Joyner-Kersee won by nearly 400 points.

Jackie's First Love

While she celebrated her victory, Joyner-Kersee stayed focused on her next task. Despite the fact that she stood head and shoulders above the rest of the world in the event, Joyner-Kersee never thought of herself as a heptathlete. She was a long jumper. The long jump had always been her favorite event, and no matter what success she achieved in any other event, it always would be. "I care about long jump the way Maya Angelou cares about her poetry and Whitney Houston cares about her voice,"[82] she once remarked.

Jackie knew that the long-jump competition would be much fiercer than she had faced in the heptathlon. No American woman had ever won the event since it was introduced to the Olympics in 1948. Among her competitors at Seoul were the world-record holder Galina Chistyakova of the Soviet Union and Heike Drechsler of East Germany, who had won twenty-seven meets in a row before losing to Joyner-Kersee in 1987.

Chistyakova opened the competition with a leap of 7.11 meters. Neither Drechsler nor Joyner-Kersee could come close to that on their first jump. Drechsler loosened up in the third round to grab the lead with a leap of 7.18 meters. Joyner-Kersee nearly matched her by jumping 7.16.

Hampered by her own injury problems, Chistyakova could not improve on her first try. Drechsler continued to apply the pressure to her rivals by soaring 7.22 meters on her fourth jump. Momentarily thrown off her concentration, Jackie fouled in round four.

As she prepared for round five, her husband-coach gave her a pep talk. He reminded her to concentrate on lifting her knees high. "You have a 7.40 in you,"[83] he told her. Jackie pounded down the runway and hit the takeoff board almost perfectly. She arched high in the air, lifted her knees, and extended her legs far forward. As soon as she hit the sand, she knew she had made a good leap. But she could hardly believe it when officials announced the distance as 7.40 meters. She had hit her husband's target exactly to claim the Olympic record and the gold medal that meant the most to her.

Courageous Finish

The 1992 Olympics in Barcelona, Spain, were more of a coronation than a competition for Joyner-Kersee in the heptathlon. Everyone knew she was the greatest female athlete in the world,

Jackie Joyner-Kersee won her second gold medal of the 1988 Games in her favorite event, the long jump.

and the event was little more than a demonstration of why. Although her performances tailed off slightly in most areas from 1988, she won the heptathlon easily with 7,044 points. Drechsler, however, came back to get the better of her in the long jump, and Jackie had to settle for third.

After Barcelona, the battle-scarred veteran of the U.S. track team continued to train, fighting through the severe asthma attacks that almost killed her at the 1995 U.S. National Championships. At the age of thirty-four, she found it increasingly difficult to stay injury-free while running the punishing workouts she needed to stay on top, but she wanted to finish her Olympic career in style in Atlanta, before the fans of her home country.

She fought through an ankle injury to earn spots in both the heptathlon and long jump at the 1996 Olympics. But three weeks before the Games, she suffered a severe pull in her right thigh. In the heptathlon hurdle race, she reinjured it but finished the race. Although she tried to go on to the high-jump pit, Bob pulled her aside. "I've watched you for twelve years give everything you've got," he said. "I'm no longer going to allow you to do this. . . . [T]his isn't a coach-athlete thing. This is your husband telling you it's time to go."[84] Tearfully Jackie dropped out of the heptathlon.

But she insisted on making one last try in the long jump. Forced to favor her throbbing leg, she could do no better than sixth place through the first five rounds. On her final jump, she decided to give it everything she had. Fighting back the pain, she somehow coaxed a monster jump out of the leg—enough to take the bronze medal.

Fans and competitors told her it was the most courageous performance they had ever seen in track and field. No one at the Games received a more thunderous ovation than Jackie Joyner-Kersee upon accepting her third-place medal.

Legacy

Dwight Stones, a former world-record holder in the high jump, declared, "There's no argument that she [Jackie] is the greatest female athlete of all time."[85] The heptathlon is considered the most rigorous test of all-around athletic ability for women, and from 1984 to 1996, Joyner-Kersee won every heptathlon she entered. She won two Olympic gold medals in the event and accumulated the six highest scores in history. In addition, she became the first woman from the United States to win the Olympic long jump.

As inspiring as her athletic skill were her courage and gritty determination. She fought against difficult odds to get to the Olympics in the first place, and she competed with almost fanatical determination once she got there. "I remember where I came from," she once said, reflecting on her career. "If young girls see the environment I grew up in, and my dreams and goals came true, they will realize that their dreams and goals might also come true."[86]

NOTES

Chapter 1: The Struggle for Acceptance

1. Quoted in Caroline Searle and Bryn Vaile, eds., *Official Olympic Companion.* London: Brassy's Sports, 1996, p. 2.

2. Quoted in Searle and Vaile, *Official Olympic Companion,* p. 2.

3. Quoted in Allen Guttman, *Women's Sports: A History.* New York: Columbia University Press, 1991, p. 134.

4. Quoted in Guttman, *Women's Sports,* p. 163.

5. Quoted in Lewis H. Carlson and John J. Fogarty, *Tales of Gold.* Chicago: Contemporary Press, 1987, p. 15.

6. Quoted in Guttman, *Women's Sports,* p. 188.

7. Quoted in Louise Mead Tricard, *American Women's Track & Field.* Jefferson, NC: McFarland, 1996, p. 176.

8. Quoted in Carlson and Fogarty, *Tales of Gold,* p. 58.

9. Quoted in Guttman, *Women's Sports,* p. 140.

10. Quoted in *Track & Field, The New York Times Encyclopedia of Sports,* Vol. 4. New York: Arno, 1979, p. 73.

11. Quoted in Tricard, *American Women's Track & Field,* p. 403.

12. Quoted in David Wallechinsky, *The Complete Book of the Olympics.* Boston: Little, Brown, 1991, p. 143.

13. Quoted in Douglas Collins, *Olympic Dreams.* New York: Universe Press, 1996, p. 221.

Chapter 2: Sonja Henie

14. Quoted in Lissa Smith, ed., *Nike Is a Goddess.* New York: Atlantic Monthly Press, 1998, p. 163.

15. Quoted in *Grace to Glory: A Century of Women in the Olympics.* Chicago: Triumph Books, 1996, p. 29.

16. Quoted in *Winter Sports, The New York Times Encyclopedia of Sports,* Vol. 9. New York: Arno, 1979, p. 14.

17. Quoted in *Winter Sports,* p. 14.

18. Quoted in *Winter Sports,* p. 15.

19. Quoted in *Winter Sports,* p. 22.

20. Quoted in *Winter Sports,* p. 41.

21. Quoted in Robert Condon, *Great Women Athletes of the 20th Century*. Jefferson, NC: McFarland, 1991, p.18.

Chapter 3: Babe Didrikson

22. Quoted in Tricard, *American Women's Track & Field*, p. 197.

23. Quoted in Harvey Frommer, *Olympic Controversies*. New York: Franklin Watts, 1987, p. 53.

24. Quoted in Tricard, *American Women's Track & Field*, p. 196.

25. Quoted in Tricard, *American Women's Track & Field*, p. 174.

26. Quoted in *Grace to Glory*, p. 34.

27. Quoted in *Track & Field*, p. 67.

28. Quoted in Tricard, *American Women's Track & Field*, p. 191.

29. Quoted in Carlson and Fogarty, *Tales of Gold*, p. 108.

30. Quoted in Tricard, *American Women's Track & Field*, p. 198.

31. Quoted in Carlson and Fogarty, *Tales of Gold*, p. 108.

32. Quoted in *Track & Field*, p. 72.

33. Guttman, *Women's Sports*, p. 14.

Chapter 4: Fanny Blankers-Koen

34. Quoted in *Grace to Glory*, p. 33.

35. Quoted in Janet Wollum, *Outstanding Women Athletes*. Phoenix: Oryx, 1992, p. 79.

36. Quoted in Smith, *Nike Is a Goddess*, p. 13.

37. Quoted in *Grace to Glory*, p. 43.

38. Wallechinsky, *Complete Book of the Olympics*, p. 148.

39. Quoted in Condon, *Great Women Athletes*, p. 70.

40. Quoted in Wallechinsky, *Complete Book of the Olympics*, p. 144.

41. Quoted in Allen Guttman, *The Olympics: A History of the Modern Games*. Chicago: University of Illinois Press, 1992, p. 82.

42. Quoted in Guttman, *Women's Sports*, p. 200.

Chapter 5: Dawn Fraser

43. Quoted in *Grace to Glory*, p. 51.

44. Quoted in *Sports Illustrated*, "Dawn Keeps Churning Along," February 17, 1964, p. 28.

45. Quoted in "Dawn Keeps Churning Along," p. 28.

46. Quoted in *Time*, "New Dawn Down Under," March 7, 1960, p. 62.

47. Quoted in "Dawn Keeps Churning Along," p. 28.

48. Quoted in "Dawn Keeps Churning Along," p. 27.

49. Quoted in "Dawn Keeps Churning Along," p. 27.

Chapter 6: Lydia Skoblikova

50. Quoted in Israel Shenker, "Curls and Cold Steel," *Sports Illustrated,* January 27, 1964, p .40.

51. Quoted in Baruch Hazan, *Olympic Sports and Propaganda Games.* Moscow, 1980. Reprint, New Brunswick, NJ: Transaction Books, 1982, p. 36.

52. Quoted in Yuri Brokhin, *The Big Red Machine.* New York: Random House, 1978, p. 128.

53. Quoted in Shenker, "Curls and Cold Steel," p. 40.

54. Quoted in Shenker, "Curls and Cold Steel," p. 40.

55. Quoted in Shenker, "Curls and Cold Steel," p. 40.

56. Quoted in Shenker, "Curls and Cold Steel," p. 40.

57. Shenker, "Curls and Cold Steel," p. 40.

58. Quoted in Dan Jenkins, "Russian Blades and Fast French Skis," *Sports Illustrated,* February 10, 1964, p. 20.

59. Quoted in *Time,* "The Olympics," February 7, 1964, p. 84.

60. Quoted in Jenkins, "Russian Blades," p. 20.

61. Quoted in Jenkins, "Russian Blades," p. 20.

Chapter 7: Nadia Comaneci

62. Quoted in Guttman, *The Olympics,* p. 68.

63. Quoted in Wollum, *Outstanding Women Athletes,* p. 87.

64. Quoted in Rebecca Nelson and Marie MacNee, eds., *The Olympic Fact Book.* Detroit: Visible Ink, 1996, p. 317.

65. Quoted in Joan Ryan, *Little Girls in Pretty Boxes.* New York: Warner, 1995, p. 209.

66. Quoted in Smith, *Nike Is a Goddess,* p. 230.

67. Quoted in Ryan, *Little Girls in Pretty Boxes,* p. 215.

68. Quoted in Guttman, *The Olympics,* p. 148.

69. Condon, *Great Women Athletes,* p. 77.

70. Quoted in Wollum, *Outstanding Women Athletes,* p. 88.

71. Quoted in Smith, *Nike Is a Goddess,* p. 226.

72. Quoted in Smith, *Nike Is a Goddess,* p. 226.

73. Quoted in Wallechinksy, *Complete Book of the Olympics,* p. 380.

74. Quoted in Ryan, *Little Girls in Pretty Boxes,* p. 24.

Chapter 8: Jackie Joyner-Kersee

75. Jackie Joyner-Kersee with Sonja Steptoe, *A Kind of Grace*. New York: Warner, 1997, p. 49.

76. Quoted in Wallechinsky, *Complete Book of the Olympics*, p. 183.

77. Quoted in Condon, *Great Women Athletes*, p. 19.

78. Quoted in Collins, *Olympic Dreams*, p. 254.

79. Joyner-Kersee, *A Kind of Grace*, p. 39.

80. Joyner-Kersee, *A Kind of Grace*, p. 49.

81. Quoted in Fred McMane and Catherine Wolf, *The Worst Day I Ever Had*. Boston: Little, Brown, 1991, p. 47.

82. Quoted in Smith, *Nike Is a Goddess*, p. 28.

83. Quoted in Wallechinsky, *Complete Book of the Olympics*, p. 172.

84. Joyner-Kersee, *A Kind of Grace*, p. 6.

85. Quoted in Joyner-Kersee, *A Kind of Grace*, p. 6.

86. Quoted in Condon, *Great Women Athletes*, p. 22.

FOR FURTHER READING

Nathan Aaseng, *Great Winter Olympic Moments*. Minneapolis: Lerner, 1990. Profiles of those events in Winter Olympic history that were especially captivating, including several women champions.

Dave Anderson, *Story of the Olympics*. New York: William Morrow, 1996. Brief, readable episodes of Olympic lore.

Harvey Frommer, *Olympic Controversies*. New York: Franklin Watts, 1987. The Olympics have had their share of emotionally charged moments, some of which involved the top women athletes. This book samples some of the more memorable of those incidents.

Bud Greenspan, *100 Greatest Moments in Olympic History*. Los Angeles: General Publishing, 1995. Capsule descriptions of the most outstanding performances in the Olympics.

Dan Gutman, *Gymnastics*. New York: Puffin, 1995. Includes profiles of Nadia Comaneci and many other star Olympic gymnasts.

Geri Harrington, *Jackie Joyner-Kersee: Champion Athlete*. New York: Chelsea House, 1995. Easy-to-read biography with emphasis on the athlete's struggles to cope with asthma and overcome poverty.

Fred McMane and Catherine Wolf, *The Worst Day I Ever Had*. Boston: Little, Brown, 1991. This unique book asks star athletes, including Jackie Joyner-Kersee, to relate some of the low spots in their careers and in doing so offers inspiration to young readers to learn the lessons of defeat and to persevere.

WORKS CONSULTED

Books

Yuri Brokhin, *The Big Red Machine*. New York: Random House, 1978. A behind-the-scenes look at the often mysterious world of Soviet athletes during the Cold War.

Lewis H. Carlson and John J. Fogarty, *Tales of Gold*. Chicago: Contemporary Press, 1987. First-person accounts by Olympic participants of their experiences at the Games.

Douglas Collins, *Olympic Dreams*. New York: Universe Press, 1996. Takes a more personal view than some histories of athletes' quests for gold.

Robert Condon, *Great Women Athletes of the 20th Century*. Jefferson, NC: McFarland, 1991. Brief summaries of the careers of the most influential female athletes of the past century.

Grace to Glory: A Century of Women in the Olympics. Chicago: Triumph Books, 1996. Well-illustrated chronicle of the growing involvement of women in the Olympics.

Allen Guttman, *The Olympics: A History of the Modern Games*. Chicago: University of Illinois Press, 1992. Straightforward historical account.

———, *Women's Sports: A History*. New York: Columbia University Press, 1991. Thorough and readable account of the advances of women's sport in the twentieth century.

Baruch Hazan, *Olympic Sports and Propaganda Games*. Moscow, 1980. Reprint, New Brunswick, NJ: Transaction Books, 1982. Scholarly examination of the mix of international politics and sport at the Moscow Olympics.

Jackie Joyner-Kersee with Sonja Steptoe, *A Kind of Grace*. New York: Warner, 1997. Interesting first-person account of the athlete's difficult childhood and Olympic challenges.

Rebecca Nelson and Marie MacNee, eds., *The Olympic Fact Book*. Detroit: Visible Ink, 1996. A basic almanac of the Olympics.

Joan Ryan, *Little Girls in Pretty Boxes*. New York: Warner, 1995. Scathing indictment of the pressures and manipulations placed upon young Olympic hopefuls in women's gymnastics and figure skating.

Caroline Searle and Bryn Vaile, eds., *Official Olympic Companion*. London: Brassy's Sports, 1996. Another almanac that also includes brief vignettes of select athletes.

Lissa Smith, ed., *Nike Is a Goddess*. New York: Atlantic Monthly Press, 1998. One of the most complete examinations of women's issues in the context of sport.

Track & Field, The New York Times Encyclopedia of Sports, Vol. 4. New York: Arno, 1979. A compilation of actual *New York Times* articles reporting on the most influential events of track and field.

Louise Mead Tricard, *American Women's Track & Field*. Jefferson, NC: McFarland, 1996. Thorough history of women in the running, throwing, and jumping competitions.

David Wallechinsky, *The Complete Book of the Olympics*. Boston: Little, Brown, 1991. The most authoritative listing of Olympic winners; often includes brief stories about the competition and/or the athletes who participated.

Winter Sports, The New York Times Encyclopedia of Sports, Vol. 9. New York: Arno, 1979. A compilation of actual *New York Times* articles reporting on the most influential events of cold-weather sports.

Janet Wollum, *Outstanding Women Athletes*. Phoenix: Oryx, 1992. Straightforward accounts of star athletes.

Periodicals

Dan Jenkins, "Russian Blades and Fast French Skis," *Sports Illustrated*, February 10, 1964.

Israel Shenker, "Curls and Cold Steel," *Sports Illustrated*, January 27, 1964.

Sports Illustrated, "Dawn Keeps Churning Along," February 17, 1964.

Time, "New Dawn Down Under," March 7, 1960.

Time, "The Olympics," February 7, 1964.

PICTURE CREDITS

Cover photos: (center) Reuters/Charles Platiau/Archive Photos, (top right) Archive Photos, (bottom right) Express Newspapers/Archive Photos, (bottom left) Underwood & Underwood/Corbis

AP Photo, 43, 49, 53, 59, 60, 64, 67, 68, 75, 77, 80, 81, 90, 93, 95

Bettmann/Corbis, 9, 11, 20, 22, 28, 34, 37, 38, 46, 50, 55, 71, 72, 82, 87, 88

FPG Inc., 24, 30, 33, 41, 56

Hulton-Deutsch/Corbis, 13, 14, 15

Library of Congress, 44

Reuters NewsMedia Inc./Corbis, 85

Underwood & Underwood/Corbis, 18, 27

ABOUT THE AUTHOR

Nathan Aaseng is the author of more than 150 books for young readers on a variety of subjects, including more than 40 on sports topics. He lives in Eau Claire, WI, and in 1999 was a winner of the Wisconsin Library Association's Notable Wisconsin Author Award.